LYCOS PERSONAL
INTERNET GUIDE

Michael Miller

201 West 103rd Street, Indianapolis, Indiana 46290

LYCOS PERSONAL INTERNET GUIDE

Copyright© 1999 by Que® Corporation.

All rights reserved. No part of this book shall be reproduced, stored in a retrieval system, or transmitted by any means, electronic, mechanical, photocopying, recording, or otherwise, without written permission from the publisher. No patent liability is assumed with respect to the use of the information contained herein. Although every precaution has been taken in the preparation of this book, the publisher and author assume no responsibility for errors or omissions. Neither is any liability assumed for damages resulting from the use of the information contained herein.

International Standard Book Number: 0-7897-1831-6

Library of Congress Catalog Card Number: 98-86987

Printed in the United States of America

First Printing: 1999

00   99   4   3   2   1

TRADEMARKS

All terms mentioned in this book that are known to be trademarks or service marks have been appropriately capitalized. Que cannot attest to the accuracy of this information. Use of a term in this book should not be regarded as affecting the validity of any trademark or service mark.

EXECUTIVE EDITOR
Jim Minatel

DEVELOPMENT EDITOR
John Sleeva

MANAGING EDITOR
Thomas F. Hayes

COPY EDITOR
Victoria Elzey

TECHNICAL EDITOR
Bill Bruns

INDEXER
Angela Williams

PROOFREADER
Megan Wade

PRODUCTION
Cyndi Davis-Hubler

COVER DESIGNER
Jay Corpus

BOOK DESIGNER
Louisa Klucznik

ABOUT THE AUTHOR

Michael Miller has been an active participant in the publishing industry since 1987, when he first joined Que Corporation. He currently serves as Vice President of Business Strategy for Macmillan Publishing, where he helps guide the company's overall vision and strategy. He has also authored or co-authored 25 nonfiction books that, together, have sold more than 600,000 copies and have been reprinted in more than a dozen languages. His most recent books are *Teach Yourself MORE Windows 98* and *Webster's New World Vocabulary of Success*.

DEDICATION

To my brother-in-law, Dennis Hauser, who has never had a book dedicated to him before—now quit complaining!

ACKNOWLEDGMENTS

Thanks to John Pierce for thinking of me for this book, and to the entire editorial team for working their usual magic.

TABLE OF CONTENTS

TELL US WHAT YOU THINK!

As the reader of this book, you are our most important critic and commentator. We value your opinion and want to know what we're doing right, what we could do better, what areas you'd like to see us publish in, and any other words of wisdom you're willing to pass our way.

As the Executive Editor for the General Desktop Applications team at Macmillan Computer Publishing, I welcome your comments. You can fax, email, or write me directly to let me know what you did or didn't like about this book—as well as what we can do to make our books stronger.

Please note that I cannot help you with technical problems related to the topic of this book, and that due to the high volume of mail I receive, I might not be able to reply to every message.

When you write, please be sure to include this book's title and author as well as your name and phone or fax number. I will carefully review your comments and share them with the author and editors who worked on the book.

Fax: 317-817-7070

E-mail: internet@mcp.com

Mail: Executive Editor
            General Desktop Applications
            Macmillan Computer Publishing
            201 West 103rd Street
            Indianapolis, IN 46290 USA

PART I

GETTING CONNECTED TO THE INTERNET

CHAPTER 1

FINDING AND CONNECTING TO AN INTERNET SERVICE PROVIDER

Before you can explore the wonders of the Internet, you first have to connect your computer to the Internet. You do this by using your PC's modem to dial up, over normal phone lines, to a company that provides Internet access. These companies, called *Internet Service Providers* (or ISPs), connect your dial-up signal directly to the Internet, thus enabling you to contact any other computer in the world that is also connected to the Internet.

> **TIP**
>
> While you're connected to your ISP, your phone line is busy, which means that you can't place or receive normal telephone calls while you're surfing the Internet. If you use the Internet a lot, you may want to invest in a second phone line just for your modem.

FINDING AN ISP

There are thousands of Internet Service Providers in America alone, some of them large and national in scope, many of them smaller and local. You can find ISPs listed in your local yellow pages, in local computer magazines and newspapers, and at various online sites.

TIP

For a comprehensive listing of both local and national ISPs, go to clnet's Ultimate Guide to Internet Service Providers at www.cnet.com/Content/Reviews/Compare/ISP or to Internet.com's Definitive ISP Buyer's Guide at thelist.iworld.com.

Here are some things to keep in mind when you're looking for an ISP:

➤ Do they have a local dial-up number? (You don't want to incur long distance charges every time you surf the Internet.)

➤ Do they have a local or toll-free technical support number? (If you run into problems, you'll need technical support.)

➤ What are the hours for their technical support? (Don't ask me why, but chances are you'll have connection problems outside of normal business hours.)

➤ What is their monthly charge or hourly rate? (If you think you'll be online a lot—you probably will—opt for a flat monthly rate; if you only expect to connect occasionally, consider a per-hour charge.)

➤ How busy are they? (Ask other subscribers how often they get a busy signal when they dial in; a growing ISP with too little capacity can be difficult to connect to during busy times of the day.)

➤ At what speeds can they connect? (Make sure their connect speeds match your modem speed; for example, some ISPs don't yet offer 56K connection speeds even though many newer modems can run this fast.)

Once you create an account with an ISP, you can then proceed to create a new Internet connection for that ISP on your personal computer.

CHOOSING LYCOS ONLINE AS YOUR ISP

Lycos, one of the premier portals to the Internet, also offers ISP service through *Lycos Online*. Lycos Online is a joint venture between Lycos and AT&T WorldNet, offering Internet connections for Windows 95 and Windows 98 users for as low as $12.95 per month.

In addition to the standard Internet connection, Lycos Online offers free email; free chat services; free online games; free personalized news, weather, and sports; and a free personalized home page. You can sign up with Lycos Online in one of two ways:

➤ Call 1-888-TRY-LYCOS (1-888-879-5926—you can drop the final "s") and request the free connection software on CD-ROM.

➤ Go to the Lycos Online Web page at www.lycos.com/att/member.html and either download the connection software or request the software on CD-ROM.

Once you have the connection software, follow the instructions to configure your PC for Lycos Online, register your new account, and get connected!

SETTING UP YOUR PC FOR A NEW ISP ACCOUNT

Before you create a new Internet connection with any Internet Service Provider (including Lycos Online), you need to gather various pieces of information from your ISP:

➤ The area code and telephone number of your ISP (their dial-up number, *not* their voice number!)

➤ Your user name and password as assigned by your ISP

➤ Your email address (in the form of *xxx@xxx.xxx*) as assigned by your ISP

➤ The names of your ISP's incoming and outgoing email servers (with some ISPs, the incoming and outgoing servers may be the same)

➤ Your email POP account name and password as assigned by your ISP

➤ The name of your ISP's news server

➤ If your ISP offers LDAP "white pages" service (not all do), the name of your ISP's LDAP server

---

TIP

Don't get confused by all the initials in the preceding list. **POP** stands for **P**ost **O**ffice **P**rotocol, which is how your ISP's email

---

server is identified on the Internet. **LDAP** stands for **L**ightweight **D**irectory **A**ccess **P**rotocol, which is a way to access directory services on the Internet.

Once you have that information, the easiest way to create a new Internet connection is by using the Internet Connection Wizard found in Internet Explorer 4 or in Microsoft Windows 98. Just follow these steps:

T I P

If you're *not* using Windows 98 or Internet Explorer 4—if you're using an older version of Windows, for example, or connecting from a Macintosh—you'll need to follow a different set of instructions to configure your computer for your ISP. The best thing to do is to ask your ISP for specific set-up instructions; in many cases, the ISP will supply you with its own installation software.

1. Open the Internet Connection Wizard (either by clicking the desktop icon, or by clicking the Windows Start button, selecting <u>P</u>rograms, selecting Internet Explorer, and then selecting Connection Wizard).

2. When the first screen of the wizard appears (as shown in Figure 1.1), select **I Want to Sign Up and Configure My Computer for a New Internet Account**.

3. Follow the instructions in the wizard to enter your account information and complete your new Internet connection.

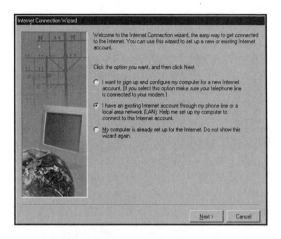

FIGURE 1.1
Use the Internet Connection Wizard to create a new Internet connection.

If you're using Windows 95 (and not using Internet Explorer 4 as your browser), you don't have the Internet Connection Wizard installed on your system. Instead, you'll need to create a new Dial-Up Networking connection manually. Consult your operating system manual or the online Help system for instructions on how to do this.

CONNECTING TO THE INTERNET VIA YOUR ISP

Once you've created the Internet connection for your ISP account, you can connect to the Internet in one of two ways:

➤ Launch any Internet application (Internet Explorer, Netscape Navigator, Outlook Express, and so on.) and Windows will automatically dial your ISP and establish a connection.

➤ Launch your Internet connection via Dial-Up Networking—just click the Windows Start button, select Programs, select Accessories, select Communications, and then select Dial-Up Networking. When the Dial-Up Networking window appears, click the icon for your ISP; when the Connect To dialog box appears, fill in your User Name and Password and click the Connect button. Once you're connected to your ISP, you can then launch any of your Internet applications.

CONNECTING TO THE INTERNET VIA AMERICA ONLINE

Using an ISP is only one way to connect to the Internet. You can also connect to the Internet via a commercial online service, such as America Online (AOL). In addition to a gateway to the Internet, America Online also offers proprietary content and communications services, such as channels and chat rooms (see Figure 1.2).

If you use America Online to connect to the Internet, you can use AOL's built-in Internet applications, or launch third-party applications (such as Internet Explorer or Netscape Navigator) on top of the AOL software. Many users like AOL because of its ease-of-use—and because of how easy it is to establish an account and get connected.

To open an account with America Online, contact them via telephone at 800-827-6364 or via the Web at www.aol.com.

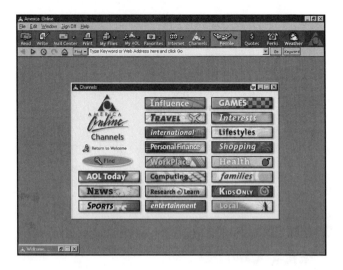

FIGURE 1.2
America Online offers a variety of specialized content in addition to an Internet gateway—click the Internet button on the toolbar to access the Internet.

ONCE YOU'RE CONNECTED...

Getting connected to the Internet is only the first step. Once you're connected, you need to launch appropriate Internet applications software, such as a Web browser or an email program. For more information, turn to Chapter 2, "Finding and Installing Your Internet Software."

CHAPTER 2

FINDING AND INSTALLING YOUR INTERNET SOFTWARE

After you've established an account with an Internet Service Provider and created a new Internet connection, you need to find and install the Internet software you need to complete your Internet tasks.

There are a variety of different Internet applications you may want to consider:

➤ **Web browser.** You use a Web browser program—such as Internet Explorer or Netscape Navigator—to view pages and sites on the World Wide Web.

➤ **Email.** An email program lets you send and receive electronic mail messages.

➤ **Newsreader.** Newsreaders let you read and post articles to USENET newsgroups.

➤ **Chat.** Chat programs let you "chat"—using real-time electronic messages—with other Internet users.

➤ **FTP.** FTP programs let you quickly download software programs from other computers connected to the Internet, as well as upload your own files to other computers.

Many of these applications can be downloaded for free or nominal charge from the Internet; others may have to be purchased at a traditional software retailer. Read on to discover where to find these necessary applications.

TIP

You may already have some of these applications. If you've recently purchased a new computer, chances are a Web browser and email program came pre-loaded on your hard disk. If you've recently installed Windows 98, it comes with a Web browser (Internet Explorer) and email program (Outlook Express) built-in. And some ISPs provide you with a disk or CD-ROM of their recommended software programs when you first open an account.

FINDING A WEB BROWSER

There are two major Web browsers available today: Microsoft's **Internet Explorer** and Netscape's **Navigator**. Both function in similar fashion, and both include similar features. Which you use is a matter of personal choice.

You can download **Internet Explorer** from Microsoft's Web site at www.microsoft.com/ie/. Installation is interactive; that is, you're led step by step through the installation after the software has been downloaded. If you prefer to skip the rather long download, you can also order the software (for free) on CD-ROM from this site. See Chapter 5, "Using Internet Explorer for Web Surfing," to learn how to use Internet Explorer.

You can download **Netscape Navigator** from Netscape's Web site at www.netscape.com/computing/download/

`index.html`. Netscape offers several different versions of their software, including free and paid versions of Navigator. (The paid version includes some degree of technical support; the free version doesn't.) Choose which version to download, then launch the installation program to install the software on your PC. See Chapter 6, "Using Netscape Navigator for Web Surfing," to learn how to use Netscape Navigator.

T I P

Both Internet Explorer and Netscape Navigator can be downloaded as simple Web browsers or as complete Internet application suites. If you choose the full installation of Internet Explorer, you'll also receive **Outlook Express** (an email and newsreader program) and, if you so select, **Microsoft Chat** and several other add-ons. If you choose to download the complete **Netscape Communicator** suite, you'll receive the Netscape Navigator browser, the **Netscape Messenger** email/newsreader program, the **Instant Messenger** chat program, and several other add-ons. Most users choose to install a complete suite from a single software publisher; it's probably the easiest way to get up-and-running in one fell swoop.

FINDING AN EMAIL PROGRAM

There are three major Internet email programs in use today; two of them can be downloaded with the Microsoft Internet Explorer or Netscape Communicator applications suites. All three programs (**Outlook Express**, **Netscape Messenger**, and **Eudora**) operate in similar fashion, although their feature sets differ slightly.

TIP

Do not confuse Internet email programs with more corporate-oriented network email programs, such as Lotus cc:mail or Microsoft Outlook—which is a more complete program than Outlook Express.

You can download **Outlook Express** from Microsoft's Web site at www.microsoft.com/ie/download/. Just choose the Outlook Express option and follow the on-screen instructions for your specific setup. See Chapter 21, "Using Outlook Express for Email," to learn how to use Outlook Express to send and receive email.

You can download **Netscape Messenger** from Netscape's Web site at www.netscape.com/computing/download/index.html. Just choose to download the complete Netscape Communicator suite, and Messenger will be included in the software download. See Chapter 22, "Using Netscape Messenger for Email," to learn how to use Netscape Messenger to send and receive email.

You can download **Eudora** from the Macmillan Computer Publishing Web site at www.mcp.com/resources/geninternet/frame_tucows.html. Just select your specific computing platform (Windows 95, Windows NT, and so on), then select Email Clients (in the E-Mail Tools section) and click on either Eudora Lite (a trimmed-down shareware version) or Eudora Pro (the full-featured commercial version). Choosing Eudora Pro will cost you $39; Eudora Lite is free.

FINDING A NEWSREADER PROGRAM

The two most popular newsreader programs are also email programs: **Outlook Express** and **Netscape Messenger**. See the previous section for instructions on finding and downloading these two programs. See Chapters 25, "Using Outlook Express for Newsgroups," and 26, "Using Netscape Messenger for Newsgroups," to learn how to use Outlook Express and Netscape Messenger to read and post newsgroup articles.

There are two other newsreader programs you may want to consider. Both **Free Agent** and **NewsXpress** let you download batches of articles quickly so you can read them offline, without incurring large online connect charges.

You can find both of these programs at the Macmillan Computer Publishing Web site at www.mcp.com/resources/geninternet/frame_tucows.html. Just select your operating system, then click on News Readers (in the Network Tools section) and proceed from there.

FINDING A CHAT PROGRAM

Microsoft and Netscape both include Chat programs as part of their Internet application suites; go to www.microsoft.com/ie/download/ or www.netscape.com/computing/download/index.html to download these programs.

You may also want to consider one of several third-party Chat programs found at the Macmillan Computer

Publishing Web site at www.mcp.com/resources/geninternet/frame_tucows.html. Just click on the specific operating system you use, then select Chat IRC Clients (in the Communications section) and choose from programs such as **IRC Gold**, **mIRC**, and **PIRCH98**. (IRC stands for Internet Relay Chat, a specific Chat protocol.)

In addition, **ICQ** is a very popular *instant messaging* program. Instant messaging lets you send instant messages to anyone currently connected to the Internet, without the need for formal Chat rooms. You can download ICQ from the Macmillan Computer Publishing Web site at www.mcp.com/resources/geninternet/frame_tucows.html. Just select your operating system, then click on Chat-Messengers (in the Communications section) and select ICQ. See Chapter 30, "Instant Messaging with ICQ," to learn how to send and receive instant messages with ICQ.

TIP

You don't have to have a Chat program to chat with other Internet users. Many Web sites—such as Lycos, at chat.lycos.com—feature Web-based Chat services you can access with your Web browser. See Chapter 29, "Chatting with Lycos Chat," to learn how to use the Lycos Chat services.

FINDING AN FTP PROGRAM

While you can use a Web browser to download files from FTP sites, many users prefer to use a dedicated FTP program. (**FTP**, which stands for **F**ile **T**ransfer **P**rotocol, is sometimes faster than Web-based downloading.) My favorite FTP program is **WS-FTP**; you can download it from the Macmillan Computer Publishing Web site at

www.mcp.com/resources/geninternet/frame_tucows.html.
Just select your operating system, then click on FTP and
Archie (under Network Tools) and select either WS-FTP
FE (a freeware version) or WS-FTP Pro (a more fully
featured commercial version). Choosing WS-FTP Pro
will cost you money; WS-FTP FE is free.

AFTER YOUR APPLICATIONS ARE INSTALLED...

After you've downloaded and installed your Internet software programs, you're ready to connect to the Internet
and start surfing the Web, sending email, and posting
newsgroup articles. Before you head online, however, you
might want to check out ways to "childproof" the
Internet for the younger members of your household; just
turn to Chapter 3, "Making the Internet Safe for
Children."

CHAPTER 3

MAKING THE INTERNET SAFE
FOR CHILDREN

The Internet contains an almost limitless supply of information; some of it is good, and some of it is potentially bad. While you want your children to be able to use the Internet for fun and education, you also want to protect them from whatever harmful content they might stumble across.

The best way to make the Internet safe for your children is to surf the Net with them. There is simply no substitution for parental involvement when it comes to protecting your children.

But if you can't always be by your kids when they're surfing, you can turn to one of the numerous "kid-safe" Web sites and software programs that filter out offensive content from the Web. These options are discussed in this chapter.

Using Internet Explorer's Content Advisor

If you use Microsoft's Internet Explorer, you can take advantage of its built-in filtering capabilities. Just follow these steps to activate and use the Content Advisor.

1. Pull down the <u>V</u>iew menu, and select Internet Options.

2. When the Internet Options dialog box appears, select the Content tab.

3. To turn on the Content Advisor feature, click the <u>E</u>nable button. (When asked for your Supervisor Password, enter your Windows password.)

TIP

When you're creating passwords for your PC, make sure you assign different passwords for parents and for children—*don't* assign one general household password, or you kids will be able to access everything you can!

---

4. To adjust specific settings, click the Se<u>t</u>tings button. (When asked for your Supervisor Password, enter your Windows password.) When the Content Advisor dialog box appears (see Figure 3.1), select the Ratings tab, then choose a type of content and then adjust the slider to the desired setting. Click OK when done.

Content Advisor is only available with Microsoft's Internet Explorer 4 browser. Unfortunately, Netscape Navigator doesn't offer a similar "content filtering" feature.

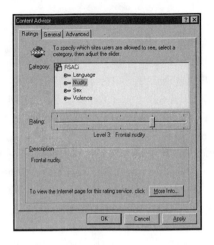

FIGURE 3.1
Use Internet Explorer's Content Advisor to filter harmful content for specific users.

Using the Lycos SafetyNet

Lycos has created a special gateway to the Web called **SafetyNet**, which stands for **S**earch **A**nd **F**ilter **E**nhanced **T**echnology for **Y**our **Net**. SafetyNet is designed to give users the ability to screen out adult content from their Web surfing; it blocks users from searching for pornographic and/or offensive words, and from accessing Lycos' Chat, email, and message board functions. If you're worried about your children seeing inappropriate responses when they search for information on the Web, SafeteyNet is the way to go.

To use SafetyNet, just follow these steps:

1. Click the Kids Safe Search link on the Lycos home page (www.lycos.com), or go directly to the registration

page at `personal.lycos.com/safetynet/`
`safetynet.asp`.

2. Read the introductory material, then click on the Continue SafetyNet Registration link.

3. When the SafetyNet Control Panel page appears, fill in all the information as appropriate. You can choose to enable the SafetyNet filter and forbid access to Chat, email, and message boards; enable the SafetyNet filter and allow access to Chat, email, and message boards; or disable the SafetyNet filter completely. Click Submit when done.

T I P

Note that SafetyNet only filters information accessed through the Lycos Web site; it does not filter information accessed at any other site. In addition, it does not affect content viewed via other programs, such as email or newsreader programs.

Once you've activated SafetyNet, you can return to the Lycos home page and surf the Web as usual. To turn off SafetyNet, click the Kids Safe Search link from the Lycos home page and select the appropriate option on the SafetyNet Control Panel page.

USING THIRD-PARTY FILTERING SOFTWARE

There are numerous software programs that let you filter inappropriate content from younger Internet users. These programs compile lists of offensive sites (or, in some instances, offensive words) and automatically block access to those sites. When unauthorized users try to access a filtered site, they receive a message informing them that the site is blocked.

All of these programs look for offensive content in various categories, including sex, language, adult situations, violence, and drugs. Table 3.1 lists the most popular filtering software available today, and how to find it.

Table 3.1   Popular Filtering Software

Software	Web Site	Phone Number
Cyber Patrol	www.cyberpatrol.com	800-828-2608
CYBERsitter	www.solidoak.com/cysitter.htm	800-388-2761
Net Nanny	www.netnanny.com	800-340-7177
SurfWatch	www.surfwatch.com	888-6SPYGLASS

ONCE YOUR CHILDREN ARE SAFE...

With the proper precautions in place, it's now time to turn your family loose on the Internet. Turn to Chapter 4, "A Quick Look at Web Pages," to learn Web surfing essentials.

PART II

SURFING THE WORLD WIDE WEB

CHAPTER 4

A QUICK LOOK AT
WEB PAGES

The *World Wide Web* is just part of the entire Internet. In particular, the Web is the part of the Internet where information is presented in a highly visual, often multimedia, format.

Information on the World Wide Web is presented in pages. A *Web page* is like a page in a book, made up of text and pictures (also called *graphics*). A Web page differs from a book page, however, in that it can include other elements, such as audio and video, and *links* to other Web pages.

Links are easy to use. Just position your cursor over a link and notice how the cursor changes shape from the normal arrow to a pointing hand. When the cursor is over the link, click your mouse button; your Web browser will automatically take you to the linked page.

A collection of Web pages is called a Web *site*. The main page at a Web site is called a *home page*, and the formal address of a Web page is called a *URL* (which stands for Uniform Resource Locator). For example, the URL for the home page of the Lycos site is www.lycos.com.

You cruise the Web using a piece of software called a *Web browser*. The two most popular browsers are Microsoft's Internet Explorer and Netscape Navigator. See Chapters 5 and 6 to learn more about these specific applications.

THE PARTS OF A WEB PAGE

How do you read a Web page? Most Web pages are made up of the same common elements, shown in Figure 4.1.

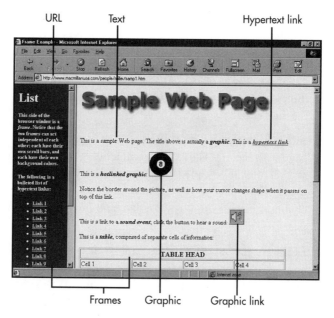

FIGURE 4.1
The elements of a Web page.

Table 4.1 explains these common elements in more detail.

Table 4.1 Web Page Elements

Element	Description
URL	The address of the current Web page.
Text	Just normal text, like you'd read in a book.
Graphic	A picture on a Web page.
Hypertext link	A text-based link to another Web page; click the underlined text to go to the linked page.
Graphic link	A graphic that, when clicked, links you to another Web page.
Frames	Some Web pages are divided into parts, each of which functions as a separate Web page.

If you're not sure what to do on a given page, first try "hovering" your mouse over various elements; sometimes a "tip box" will appear that will describe the selected element. If you hover over something that is clickable, your cursor will turn into a small hand. When this happens, go ahead and click—you never know what will happen! (And if you don't like where you go to, just click your browser's "back" button to return to the prior page.)

TIP

Sometimes Web pages can be very slow to load. This can be caused by a slow Internet connection, heavy traffic on the Internet, too many users on this specific Web site, or a Web page that includes too many large graphics. If you find that a page is taking too long to completely load—or if you get a "cannot open site" or "page not found" error—make sure you've entered the correct URL and try accessing the page again.

FANCY WEB PAGES

In addition to these common elements, some Web pages use more advanced features. It's not uncommon to encounter pages that include the following:

➤ **Animated graphics.** These are pictures that move or incorporate some sort of special effect. Normally, you don't have to do anything to view the animation; it occurs automatically.

➤ **Movies.** Yes, the Web can broadcast full-motion video. (It just takes a lot of time to download to your computer, is all.)

➤ **Sounds.** Sounds on the Web can range from simple clicks and beeps to fully orchestrated background music in the MIDI format used by professional musicians. (For more information on finding sounds on the Internet, see Chapter 13, "Searching for Pictures, Sounds, and Movies.")

➤ **Interactive applets.** Some Web sites even include interactive programs (called "applets") that let you perform specific tasks in real time. Applets are often created using special Web programming languages such as Java, Dynamic HTML, or ActiveX, and can include stock tickers, biorhythm charts, and other such utilities.

To view some of these special effects, you may need to download and install special "plug-ins" to your Web browser. In most cases you will be prompted if your browser does not currently employ these plug-ins; you can download most plug-ins from the same site where you downloaded your browser software.

ONCE YOU'VE LEARNED ABOUT WEB PAGES...

I find that cruising the Web is like browsing through an encyclopedia. Invariably when I'm reading one article in an encyclopedia, I find a reference to a related article that interests me. When I turn to the new article, I find a reference to another article, which references another article...and, before I know it, I have all 24 volumes open in front of me. When you're on the Web, it's the same sort of experience. In the course of a single session, it's not unusual to discover that you've visited more than a dozen different sites—and still have lots of interesting places to go!

So now that you've learned how to "read" Web pages, it's time to learn how to use your specific Web browser. If you're using Internet Explorer, turn to Chapter 5; if you're using Netscape Navigator, turn to Chapter 6.

CHAPTER 5

USING INTERNET EXPLORER FOR WEB SURFING

Internet Explorer is the Web browser developed by Microsoft Corporation. You can install Internet Explorer on almost any computer system; it is also included free of charge as part of the Windows 98 operating system.

THE PARTS OF INTERNET EXPLORER

Internet Explorer functions like any Microsoft program, using a series of pull-down menus and toolbar buttons. Because a browser is a bit different from a word processor, however, use Figure 5.1 and Table 5.1 to learn the parts of the Internet Explorer interface.

Address box—enter
Web addresses here

Toolbar—click these buttons to
perform common functions

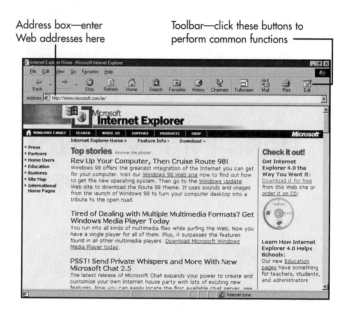

FIGURE 5.1

Microsoft's Web browser, Internet Explorer; this is Internet Explorer 4, running on Windows 98.

Table 5.1 Internet Explorer Toolbar Buttons

	Button	Operation
Back	Back	Return to the previously viewed page
Forward	Forward	View the next page
Stop	Stop	Stop loading the current page
Refresh	Refresh	Reload the current page
Home	Home	Return to your designated start page
Search	Search	Display the Search pane and initiate a Web search
Favorites	Favorites	Display the Favorites pane

Button		Operation
⚙ History	History	Display the History pane to see a list of recently viewed pages
⚡ Channels	Channels	View a list of Active Channels with specific content "pushed" to your desktop
▱ Fullscreen	Fullscreen	View Web pages in full-screen mode
✉ Mail	Mail	Launch Outlook Express to read email and newsgroup articles
🖨 Print	Print	Print the current page
✎ Edit	Edit	Display the HTML code for the current page

CONFIGURING INTERNET EXPLORER

You can change many options in Internet Explorer to make it better suit your personal needs. For example, you may want to change the color of links you have visited; or if you are concerned about security, you may want to turn on warnings when entering an unsecured site. You can change the options at any time—whether you are currently connected to the Internet or not.

To change Internet Explorer's default configuration:

1. From within Internet Explorer, pull down the View menu and select Internet Options.

2. When the Internet Options dialog box appears, configure the appropriate options.

3. After you have Internet Explorer configured as you like, click the OK button.

BASIC WEB SURFING WITH INTERNET EXPLORER

Internet Explorer enables you to quickly and easily browse the World Wide Web—just by clicking your mouse.

1. When you first launch Internet Explorer, it will load your predefined home page.

TIP

To change Internet Explorer's home page, pull down the View menu and select Internet Options. When the Internet Options dialog box appears, select the General tab and enter a new URL into the Address box in the Home Page section. (Here's an even quicker way to make the current page your start page, without opening any dialog boxes—just drag the page's icon from Internet Explorer's Address box onto the Home button on the toolbar.)

---

2. Enter a new Web address in the Address box and press Enter. Internet Explorer will load the new page.

3. Click any link on the current Web page. Internet Explorer will load the new page.

4. To return to the previous page, click the Back button. If you've backed up several pages and want to return to the page you were on last, click the Forward button.

5. To return to your start page, click the Home button.

> **TIP**
>
> Sometimes Web pages will take a long time to load—if they contain a lot of graphics, for example. If you get tired of waiting for a Web page to load, you can click the Stop button to stop the process. If you want to reload a partially loaded page, click the Refresh button.

SAVING YOUR FAVORITE WEB PAGES

When you find a Web page you like, add it to a list of Favorites within Internet Explorer. With this feature, you can access any of your favorite sites just by choosing it from the list.

To add a page to your Favorites list:

1. Go to the page you would like to add to your Favorites list.

2. Pull down the Favorites menu and select Add to Favorites.

3. When the Add Favorite dialog box appears, click No Subscription and confirm the page's Name, and then click the Create In button.

4. Select the folder where you want to place this link, and then click OK.

To view a page in your Favorites list:

1. Click the Favorites button. The browser window will automatically split into two panes, with your favorites displayed in the left pane (see Figure 5.2).

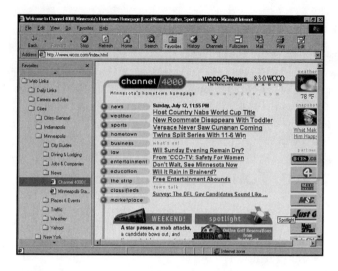

FIGURE 5.2
Click the Favorites button to display the Favorites pane; click on any link to display that page in the right pane.

2. Click any folder in the Favorites pane to display the contents of that folder.

3. Click a favorite page and that page will be displayed in the right pane.

4. Click the Favorites button again to hide the Favorites pane.

TIP

If you add a lot of pages to your Favorites list, it can become unwieldy. To reorganize the Favorites list, use your mouse to drag a favorite page into a new folder or position. To delete a favorite, just highlight it and press Delete.

ONCE YOU'VE LEARNED ABOUT INTERNET EXPLORER...

Now that you know how to use Internet Explorer, it's time to explore one of the most popular sites on the Web—just turn to Chapter 7, "Using Lycos."

CHAPTER 6

USING NETSCAPE NAVIGATOR FOR WEB SURFING

Netscape Navigator is, like Internet Explorer, a tool you use for Web browsing. Developed by Netscape Corporation, Navigator (and the entire Communicator suite) can be installed on almost any computer system.

THE PARTS OF NETSCAPE NAVIGATOR

Netscape Navigator functions in much the same manner as Internet Explorer, using a series of pull-down menus and toolbar buttons. Use Figure 6.1 and Table 6.1 to learn the parts of the Netscape Navigator interface.

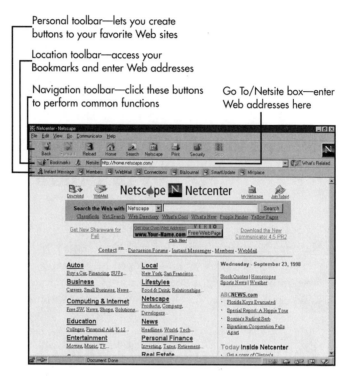

Personal toolbar—lets you create buttons to your favorite Web sites

Location toolbar—access your Bookmarks and enter Web addresses

Navigation toolbar—click these buttons to perform common functions

Go To/Netsite box—enter Web addresses here

FIGURE 6.1
Netscape's Web browser, Navigator.

Table 6.1 Toolbar Buttons

	Button	Operation
	Back	Return to the previously viewed page
	Forward	View the next page
	Reload	Reload the current page
	Home	Return to your designated start page

	Button	Operation
![Search]	Search	Load a special Netscape search page
![Netscape]	My Netscape	Display your own personal start page on Netscape's Web site
![Print]	Print	Print the current page
![Stop]	Security	Display security information about the current page and site
![What's Related]	Stop	Stop loading the current page
![Bookmarks]	Bookmarks	Display bookmarked pages
![Instant Message]	Instant Message	Launch the AOL Instant Messenger application
![None]	What's Related	Display Web pages related to the current page

TIP

AOL Instant Messenger is a utility that lets you exchange real-time messages with other Instant Messenger users.

CONFIGURING NETSCAPE NAVIGATOR

You can change many options in Netscape Navigator to make it better suit your personal needs. For example, you may want to change the color of links you have visited, or you may want to change the amount of disk space used to "cache" recently visited Web pages. You can change the options at any time—whether you are currently connected to the Internet or not.

> **TIP**
>
> A *cache* is the spare disk space that Netscape uses to store recently visited Web pages; this helps the pages load faster if you revisit them at a later date. The bigger the cache, the more pages that can be stored—but the more disk space that is used.

To change Navigator's default configuration:

1. From within Netscape Navigator, pull down the Edit menu and select Preferences.
2. When the Preferences dialog box appears, configure the appropriate options.
3. After you have Navigator configured as you like, click the OK button.

BASIC WEB SURFING WITH NETSCAPE NAVIGATOR

Netscape Navigator enables you to quickly and easily browse the World Wide Web—just by clicking your mouse.

1. When you first launch Navigator, it will load your predefined home page.

> **TIP**
>
> To change Navigator's home page, pull down the Edit menu and select Preferences. When the Preferences dialog box appears, select Navigator in the left-hand pane and enter a

new URL into the Location box in the Home Page section. If you want to make the current page your home page, click the Use Current Page button.

2. Enter a new Web address in the Go To/Netsite box and press Enter. Navigator will load the new page.

TIP

With the latest version of Navigator, you don't even have to enter the entire address. You can leave out the http://, the www., and the .com—Navigator will assume you want these in the address and add them automatically. For example, instead of entering http://www.mcp.com for Macmillan's Web site, you can just enter mcp and Navigator will do the rest.

3. Click any link on the current Web page. Navigator will load the new page.

4. To return to the previous page, click the Back button. If you've backed up several pages and want to return to the page you were at last, click the Forward button.

5. To return to your start page, click the Home button.

TIP

Sometimes Web pages will take a long time to load—if they contain a lot of graphics, for example. If you get tired of waiting for a Web page to load, you can click the Stop button to stop the process. If you want to reload a partially loaded page, click the Reload button.

BOOKMARKING YOUR FAVORITE WEB PAGES

When you find a Web page you like, add it to a list of Bookmarks within Navigator. With this feature, you can access any of your favorite sites just by choosing it from the list.

To add a page to your Bookmarks list:

1. Go to the page you would like to add to your Bookmarks list.

2. Click the Bookmarks button and select Add Bookmark.

3. If you want to add a Bookmark to a preexisting Bookmark folder, select File Bookmark, then select the folder to which you want to add.

TIP

You can also create a bookmark by dragging the "link to" icon (next to the Netsite/Go To box) and dropping it on the Bookmarks icon.

To view a page in your Bookmarks list, just click the Bookmarks button, then select the bookmark you wish to view, as shown in Figure 6.2. (Select any folder to display the contents of that folder.)

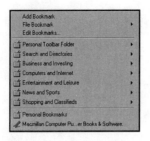

FIGURE 6.2
Click the Bookmarks button to display bookmarked pages; click on any link to display that page.

TIP

If you add a lot of pages to your Bookmarks list, it can become unwieldy. To reorganize the Bookmarks list, click the Bookmarks button and select Edit Bookmarks. Use your mouse to drag bookmarks from one location to another; to delete a bookmark, just highlight it and press Delete.

ONCE YOU'VE LEARNED ABOUT NETSCAPE NAVIGATOR...

Now that you know how to use Netscape Navigator, it's time to explore one of the most popular sites on the Web—just turn to Chapter 7, "Using Lycos."

CHAPTER 7

USING LYCOS

Lycos is one of the most popular sites on the Web.
Initially just a search engine designed to help users find
sites on the Web, Lycos has added content and services to
become a true *portal* to the Internet that is a destination
unto itself.

Many users make Lycos their home page that starts up
every time they launch their Web browser. From Lycos
you can go anywhere else on the Web—although, in
many cases, you can find what you're looking for without
ever leaving the Lycos site.

THE MANY PARTS OF WWW.LYCOS.COM

When you load the Lycos home page (www.lycos.com),
you're presented with the page shown in Figure 7.1.
From here you can search the Web, view a topic-specific
Web guide, or access a host of other services and information.

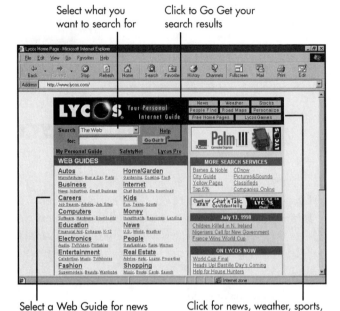

Select what you want to search for

Click to Go Get your search results

Select a Web Guide for news and features on a given topic

Click for news, weather, sports, and other special items

FIGURE 7.1

The best way to explore the Internet—Lycos!

Lycos includes many different areas—more than you might realize at first glance. Here is just a sampling of what you can find on the Lycos Web site:

➤ **Chat** (also accessible at chat.lycos.com), a collection of real-time online Chat rooms, including special celebrity Chat special events. See Chapter 29 to learn more about Lycos Chat.

➤ **City Guide** (also accessible at cityguide.lycos.com), a collection of local Web sites for cities all around the world—each site includes local news, information, and Web links. See Chapter 15 to learn more about local information online.

➤ **Classifieds** (also accessible direct at `www.lycos.com/emarket/classifieds/`), hundreds of thousands of classified ads for all types of goods and services—includes online personals ads. See Chapters 19 and 20 to learn more about using online classified ads.

➤ **Companies Online** (also accessible direct at `www.companiesonline.com`), Dun & Bradstreet's listing of detailed company information for more than 100,000 private and public companies. See Chapter 11 to learn more about searching for businesses and company information.

➤ **Free Home Pages** (also accessible at `homepager.tripod.com`), Tripod's personal Web page creation and hosting service. See Chapter 32 to learn more about Tripod and personal Web pages.

➤ **Free Software** (also accessible at `www.lycos.com/computers/miniguide/zdnet/download`), thousands of freeware and shareware programs to download, in conjunction with the ZDNet Web site. See Chapter 12 to learn more about downloading software from the Internet.

➤ **Get Email** (also accessible at `www.lycosemail.com`), Lycos' free Web-based email (called LycosMail). See Chapter 23 to learn more about LycosMail.

➤ **Kids Safe Search** (also accessible direct at `personal.lycos.com/safetynet/safetynet.asp`), a filtering system to keep inappropriate content out of the hands of younger Internet users. See Chapter 3 to learn more about making the Internet safe for children.

➤ **Lycos Online** (also accessible direct at
`www.lycos.com/att/member.html`), details about a
low-priced Internet connection service from Lycos
and AT&T. See Chapter 1 to learn more about finding and subscribing to an Internet Service Provider.

➤ **Lycos Search**, where you can search the Web and
other areas of the Internet for the information you
need. See Chapter 9 to learn more about searching
the Web with Lycos Search.

➤ **Message Boards** (also accessible at
`bbs.lycoschat.com`), special electronic boards where
you can read and post messages related to specific
topics. See Chapter 28 to learn more about Lycos
Message Boards.

➤ **My Start Page** (also accessible direct at
`personal.lycos.com`), a special home page you can
customize with the news and information you want to
see. See Chapter 8 to learn more about customized
start pages.

➤ **News** (also accessible direct at `news.lycos.com`), up-
to-the-minute news and headlines from Reuters. See
Chapter 14 to learn more about news on the Web.

➤ **Online Games** (also accessible at
`playsite.lycos.com`), a variety of online multi-player
games, such as Backgammon, Chess, and Euchre.

➤ **Pictures&Sounds** (also accessible direct at
`www.lycos.com/picturethis/`), an image gallery with
more than 40,000 free pictures and illustrations—and
a special engine to search the Web for pictures and
sounds. See Chapter 13 to learn more about searching for pictures and sounds.

➤ **Road Maps** (also accessible at www.lycos.com/roadmap.html), a service that provides maps and driving locations for locations you specify. See Chapter 16 to learn more about planning a trip online.

➤ **Search Options** (also accessible direct at lycospro.lycos.com), for more advanced and precise Web searches. See Chapter 9 for more information.

➤ **Stocks** (also accessible direct at investing.lycos.com), the latest financial and investing news, including stock quotes and charts. See Chapter 18 to learn more about managing stocks and finances online.

➤ **Top 5% Websites** (also accessible direct at point.lycos.com), a guide to the top 5% of all Web sites, as rated by Lycos' experienced reviewers.

➤ **Weather** (also accessible at weather.lycos.com), weather forecasts and maps for most U.S. and international cities. See Chapter 14 to learn more about weather on the Web.

➤ **Web Guides**, specialized pages containing news, features, and activities related to a specific topic—as well as special Community Guides that contain links to related Web pages. See the following section to learn more about Lycos Web Guides.

➤ **White Pages** (also accessible direct at www.lycos.com/peoplefind/), a variety of search services and listings to help you find people—phone numbers, addresses, email addresses, even a reverse phone number lookup. See Chapter 10 to learn more about using this People Find feature to search for people on the Internet.

> ➤ **Yellow Pages** (also accessible direct at `yp.gte.net`),
> GTE's Yellow Pages online—a great way to search
> for business phone numbers and addresses.

You can access most of these areas from the Lycos main
page (`www.lycos.com`), or directly through the URLs listed.
It's worth spending a few hours exploring the Lycos site—
it's more than just a search engine, it's your personal guide
to the Web!

TIP

If, at any time, you need help figuring out how to use Lycos,
just click the Help link on the main page (or go directly to
`www.lycos.com/help/`).

LYCOS WEB GUIDES

Perhaps the best way to start exploring Lycos is through
its Web Guides. Each Web Guide includes news and
information about a particular topic—as well as links to
related sites elsewhere on the Web. Lycos includes Web
Guides for a wide variety of topics, from Autos to Travel.

Think of a Web Guide as an online community, with
everything you need to know about a specific topic located
all in one place. Figure 7.2 shows a typical Web Guide.

Within each Web Guide are Community Guides that
point to information on the Web most relevant to the
topic on hand. This list includes those Web pages that
best match the specific topic of that Web Guide, as
decided by other Community members; when you visit
one of these recommended sites, you see a special toolbar
that lets you vote on whether or not you like the page
and think it should be in the Community Guides.

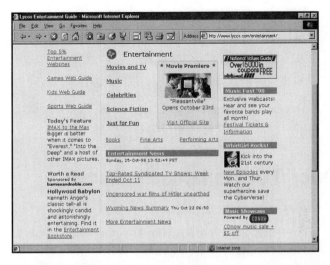

FIGURE 7.2
Lycos' Entertainment Web Guide—a community devoted to movies, television, music, and celebrities.

LOTS OF LYCOS LANGUAGES

The main Lycos site is in English, and is admittedly somewhat U.S.-centric. Fortunately for users around the world, Lycos also maintains several country-specific sites. While new international sites are coming online frequently, here are the non-U.S. sites available at the time this book was written, along with their URLs:

➤ Belgium (www.be.lycos.de)

➤ France (www.lycos.fr)

➤ Germany (www.lycos.de)

➤ Italy (www.lycos.it)

➤ Japan (www-jp.lycos.com)

➤ Netherlands (www.lycos.nl)

➤ Spain (www.es.lycos.de)

➤ Sweden (www.lycos.se)

➤ Switzerland (www.lycosch.ch)

➤ United Kingdom (www.lycos.co.uk)

You can also access many of these non-U.S. sites from links at the bottom of the main U.S. Lycos page.

ONCE YOU'VE LEARNED ABOUT LYCOS...

Now that you know all about Lycos, it's time to use Lycos Personal Guide to create your own customized start page. Just turn to Chapter 8, "Creating Your Own Customized Start Page," for more information.

CHAPTER 8

CREATING YOUR OWN
CUSTOMIZED START PAGE

Lycos is a great Web site, but it *is* kind of generic—
wouldn't it be nice if you could pick and choose those
parts of Lycos that you really like and use a lot, and put
them all together on a single customized page, just for
your personal use? Well, Lycos includes a feature that lets
you do just that—create your own personal guide to the
Internet!

CREATING YOUR PERSONAL GUIDE

When you first click on the My Start Page link on the
Lycos home page (or go directly to personal.lycos.com),
you need to personalize this page for your own specific
interests. Just follow these steps:

1. From the Personal Guide page
   (personal.lycos.com), click on the FREE: Sign up
   and personalize this page link.

2. On the registration page, enter your name, gender,
   birthdate, email address, and zip code.

3. Still on the registration page, move to the Personalize Content section and check the content you wish to appear on your main page; uncheck those items you don't want to see. Click the Continue to Personalize button to continue.

4. On the second page you get down to hard-core customization. Begin by selecting which types of news you wish to display. Note that you can select multiple Entertainment and Local news subcategories from the list boxes; just hold down the Ctrl key while you select multiple items.

5. Still on the second page, move down to the Personalize Stocks section. Enter the ticker symbols of those stocks you wish to track, separated by spaces.

6. Move to the Personalize Top 5% section, and select which categories of reviews (if any) you wish to display.

7. Move to the Personalize Favorite Links section and enter any URLs you wish to display on your personalized page.

8. Move to the Personalize Sports section. Click on the sports icons to display a full list of teams in that sport; select which teams you wish to display information about.

9. When finished, click the Submit Preferences button.

10. Your Personal Guide is now displayed, as shown in Figure 8.1. You're not done, however. Click the Content & Layout link to change the way all this content is displayed, or click the Color link to change the color scheme of your personal page.

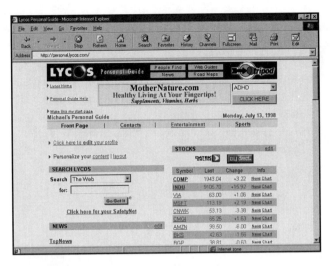

FIGURE 8.1
Your Personal Guide—fully customized!

Note that you can change the content of any section on
your personal page at any time. Just click the Edit link for
any section to make your new choices.

MAKING LYCOS PERSONAL GUIDE
YOUR HOME PAGE

Normally you have to get into some browser-specific
options to change the home pages for Internet Explorer
or Netscape Navigator. Lycos, however, makes it easy to
make your Personal Guide your default home page—just
click on the Make This My Start Page link and your
Personal Guide will become your new home page when
you launch your Web browser.

ONCE YOU'VE CREATED YOUR OWN PERSONAL GUIDE...

Now that you have your own customized start page, it's time to actually start doing things on the Internet. The most common use of the Internet is to search for information, so turn to Chapter 9, "Searching the Web with Lycos," to learn more.

PART III

SEARCHING THE INTERNET

CHAPTER 9

SEARCHING THE WEB
WITH LYCOS

The World Wide Web is made up of millions and millions of individual Web pages. Finding the one specific page you want can be like finding a needle in a haystack—unless you use the right tool to conduct your search.

The Lycos Web site (www.lycos.com) contains a search engine that lets you hunt down specific information on the Web. Using Lycos' search engine, you can find the information you want—without taking forever to find it!

TIP

The Lycos search engine is built on a special software program called *spider*. Spider software automatically roams the Web and catalogs new pages and sites as they're created. (By the way, a *lycos* is a certain type of spider—hence the name of the search engine and Web site!)

BASIC SEARCHING

While Lycos does offer more advanced search options, discussed later in this chapter, most searches can be done

directly from the main Lycos page. To initiate a basic
search of the Web, follow these steps:

1. To to the main Lycos page, at www.lycos.com. (See
Figure 9.1.)

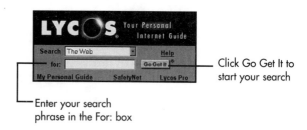

Click Go Get It to
start your search

Enter your search
phrase in the For: box

FIGURE 9.1
Searching the Web with Lycos.

2. Enter the word or phrase you wish to search for in
the For: box.

3. Click the Go Get It button (or press Enter).

Lycos will now automatically retrieve a list of Web pages
that match your search criteria. As you can see in Figure
9.2, a typical results page includes a Matching Categories
section that lists larger categories that match your query,
and a Check These Out section that offers alternative
searches (similar to the list in the Search box) for the item
you're searching for. Your actual results are listed below
these sections, under the Web Pages heading.

The results are listed in order of relevancy; the closest
matches are listed first. In addition, all matching pages
within the same site are grouped together—this way you
can skip over similar pages if necessary.

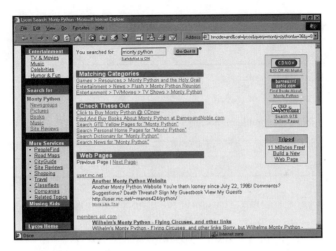

FIGURE 9.2
The results of a Lycos Web search.

To go to a page listed in the results, just click on its link.
To view similar Web pages on the selected site, click the
Similar Pages link underneath each page link; to display
the next page of results, click the Next Page link at the
bottom of the page.

FINE-TUNING YOUR SEARCH

The problem with searching the Web is that even a basic
search can return hundreds—if not thousands—of matching pages. How can you narrow your search to return
only the most relevant results?

Fortunately, Lycos has several ways for you to fine-tune
your search and return fewer—but better—results. Table
9.1 lists some of the more common commands you can
enter into the For: box to narrow your search parameters.

Table 9.1 Lycos Search Parameters

To do this:	Use this command:	Example:
Match a word *exactly*	.	monty.
Search for part of a word	$	mon$
Search for a complete phrase	" "	"monty python"
Exclude pages that contain a word	-	monty-python
Require a word on a page	+	monty+python

For example, searching for **mon$** would return pages dealing with money, monsters, and Monty Python; searching for **monty+python** would return Monty Python pages or pages about pythons owned by guys named Monty; searching for **"monty python"** would only return pages about the British comedy troupe Monty Python.

ADVANCED SEARCHING WITH LYCOS PRO SEARCH

Even using these search parameters might still return too many of the wrong results. For that reason, Lycos offers a more advanced searching method called **Lycos Pro Search**. Use Pro Search when your standard searches prove either fruitless or too fruitful.

To use Pro Search, follow these steps:

1. From the main Lycos page (www.lycos.com), click on the Search Options link to display the Lycos Pro Search page (see Figure 9.3).

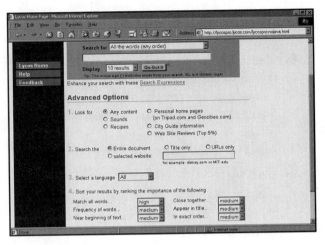

FIGURE 9.3
Use Lycos Pro Search for more advanced searches

2. Pull down the Search For box and select *how* you wish to search. (See Table 9.2 for details on each option.)

3. Enter the word or phrase to search for in the search box.

4. Pull down the Display box and select how many results to display.

5. Under the Look For... section, determine *what kind* of content you want to Look For on the Internet. (See Table 9.3 for details on these options.)

6. Under the Search The... section, determine whether you want to search the entire document (Web page), the page title only, the page URL, or all the pages on a selected Web site. (If you select to search an entire Web site, enter the main URL for that site in the box.)

7. Under the Select a Language... section, select which language (English, Spanish, etc.) you wish to search in.

8. Under the Sort Results By... section, give a ranking (low, medium, high) to the importance of each of the following search criteria: Match All Words, Frequency of Words, (words listed) Near Beginning of Text, (words) Close Together, (words as they) Appear in Title, (words) In Exact Order.

9. Click Go Get It to begin your search.

Lycos Pro Search offers you several ways to search for results, all accessible from the Search For drop-down box and explained in Table 9.2.

Table 9.2 Lycos Pro Search For Options

Option	Description
Any of the Words (OR query)	Searches for any of the listed words, in any order. For example, if you searched for **monty python**, this would return sites that only included the words monty, or the words python, or both. This is the equivalent of a standard Lycos search.
Natural Language Query	This option lets you pose a question—in natural language—to Lycos. For example, you could enter **what comedy team included john cleese?** and hope to get the correct answer. (To be honest, natural language query doesn't always work all that well.)
All the Words (any order)	Searches for pages that include all the words you listed, in any order. For example, searching for **monty python** would return sites that included the words monty and python—including where the words were used in completely different sentences.

Option	Description
All the Words (in order)	Searches for pages that include all the words you listed, as long as they appear in the order listed. For example, searching for **monty python** would return a page with the phrase "My name is Monty, and this is my Python," but would *not* return a page with the phrase "This is my Python, and his name is Monty."
All the Words (within 25 words, any order)	Searches for pages that include all the words, as long as the words are within 25 words of each other, in any order.
All the Words (within 25 words, in order)	Searches for pages that include all the words, as long as the words are within 25 words of each other *and* are used in the order specified.
All the Words (adjacent, any order)	Searches for pages where all the words listed are in a row, but not necessarily in the order listed. For example, you could search for **python monty** to return Monty Python.
The Exact Phrase	Searches for a phrase exactly as entered. For example, searching for **monty python** would only return pages about Monty Python.

In addition, Lycos Pro Search lets you search for specific types of content on the Internet, as explained in Table 9.3.

Table 9.3   Lycos Pro Look For... Options

Option	Description
Any Content	Searches the entire World Wide Web for anything you can think of
Downloads	Finds files for downloading from the Internet
News (Reuters)	Searches recent news headlines

continues

Table 9.3 continued

Option	Description
Top 5% Websites	Searches through detailed reviews of the Top 5% rated Web sites
Stock (symbol)	Displays quotes, financial information, and company news when you enter a specific stock symbol
Cities	Displays the Lycos City Guide when you enter a specific city
Dictionary	Displays definitions from *The American Heritage® Dictionary of the English Language, Third Edition*
Pictures	Finds graphics files on the Web
Recipes	Finds cooking recipes on the Web
Weather	Displays detailed forecasts when you enter a specific city
Books	Displays contents and ordering information—from Lycos partner Barnes & Noble's Web site at www.barnesandnoble.com—when you enter the title of a book
Music (artist)	Displays discography and ordering information—from Lycos partner CDnow—when you enter the name of a recording artist
Personal Home Pages	Finds user-created Web pages on the Tripod and GeoCities services
Sounds	Finds sound files on the Web
Newsgroups	Searches USENET newsgroup articles

Since Lycos Pro Search offers so many options, many users find it too complex to use for standard searches. But if you need the power for a special search, Pro Search lets you turn it all on to find the results you want!

FINDING THE *BEST* SITES WITH LYCOS TOP 5%

In addition to the Lycos and Lycos Pro search engines, Lycos also includes a directory of the best Web sites, called the Top 5%. You can access the Top 5% by clicking the Top 5% Websites link on the main Lycos page, or by going directly to point.lycos.com/categories.

The Top 5% lists the best of the Web, sorted into 18 major categories, as selected by Lycos editors. The Top 5% includes both commercial and personal sites; excellence within a category is the only criterion.

To look for a Top 5% site, you can either click on the category on the Top 5% page, or enter a search phrase in the Search Top 5% box and click Go Get It. Use the Top 5% when you value quality over quantity of results.

TIP

Once you view a Top 5% site, you can use the navigation bar at the top of the page to tell Lycos how *you* liked the site. Your opinions help determine future Top 5% lists.

ONCE YOU'VE MASTERED GENERAL SEARCHES...

Now that you've learned about how to conduct general searches on the Web with Lycos, it's time to learn about some more specific searches. Arguably, the most common type of specific search is a search for *people*, so turn to Chapter 10, "Searching for People with PeopleFind," to learn more about searching for people on the Internet.

CHAPTER 10

SEARCHING FOR PEOPLE WITH PEOPLEFIND

The Internet is a great place to find people. While you *can* search for people using the standard Lycos search engine, you'll only find them if they have their own Web page or are mentioned on someone else's Web page. A much better way to search for people on the Internet is to use a search engine specifically designed for people's names, addresses, and phone numbers, such as Lycos' PeopleFind.

SEARCHING FOR NAMES, ADDRESSES, AND PHONE NUMBERS

PeopleFind is a collection of services that let you find names, phone numbers, addresses, email addresses, and other personal information. As you can see in Figure 10.1, PeopleFind even lets you look for businesses, fax numbers, government information, and your personal horoscope! You can access PeopleFind by clicking the White Pages link on the main Lycos Web page, or by going directly to www.lycos.com/peoplefind.

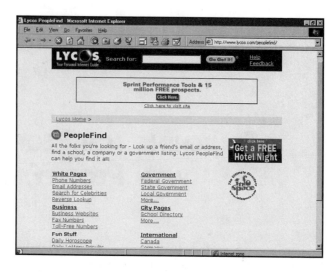

FIGURE 10.1
Use PeopleFind to search for all sorts of personal information.

To search for a person's phone number and street address, follow these steps:

1. From the main PeopleFind page, click on the Phone Numbers link (in the White Pages section).

2. When the next page appears, enter as much of the following information as you know: First Name, Last Name, City, State, and Country. If you don't know a particular item, leave it blank.

TIP

If you only know *part* of an item, enter that part. For example, if you're looking for someone named Sherry, enter **sherry**. If you're not sure whether she goes by Sherry or Sheryl, enter **sher**. If you know her first name begins with an "s"—but don't

---

know whether it's Sherry or Shannon or Susan—enter **s**. If you don't remember her first name at all, leave the First Name field blank.

3. To search in an entire metro area (including a city proper and all its suburbs), select Region/Metro Search.

4. Click Go Get It to initiate the search.

All names matching your search criteria are now displayed, as shown in Figure 10.2. Click a specific name to display complete information, including the full address, phone number, links to local information, and a neighborhood map.

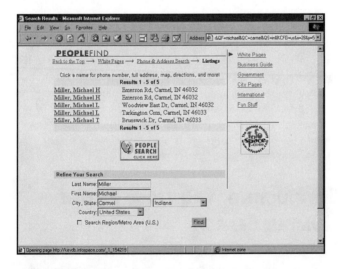

FIGURE 10.2
The results of a PeopleFind search; click on a specific name for more detailed information.

SEARCHING FOR EMAIL ADDRESSES

You can also use PeopleFind to search for a person's email address. Just follow these steps:

1. From the PeopleFind page, click the `Email Addresses` link.

2. When the next page appears, enter as much of the following information as you know—First Name, Last Name, City, State, and Country. If you don't know a particular item, leave it blank.

3. Click Go Get It to initiate the search.

The results of your search are now displayed. Click the email address next to a name to send an email message to that person.

TIP

PeopleFind's email search will only return addresses that have been listed with Lycos; for every one email address returned, there may be dozens more that are not listed. This is a problem with searching for email addresses—since there is really no central repository for email addresses on the Internet, any search for an email address is likely to come up empty.

CONDUCTING A REVERSE PHONE NUMBER SEARCH

If you know a phone number but not a name or address, you can conduct a "reverse search" and find out who is connected to that phone number—and where they live. You can also connect names to street addresses and email addresses, and find out what region is connected to what area code.

TIP

To protect personal privacy, unlisted numbers are not accessible from any of PeopleFind's search offerings.

Follow these steps to conduct a reverse search on a known piece of information:

1. From the PeopleFind page, click the Reverse Lookup link.

2. To find out who owns a known telephone number, enter the phone number in the appropriate box in the Reverse Phone and Fax Number section and click Go Get It.

3. To find out who lives at a known address, enter the address in the Reverse Address section and click Go Get It.

4. To find out where a specific area code is, enter the area code in the Reverse Area Code section and click Go Get It.

5. To find out who owns a known email address, enter the email address in the Reverse Email section and click Go Get It.

SEARCHING FOR PERSONAL HOME PAGES

If a person has a personal Web page on either the Tripod or GeoCities services, you can use Lycos to find that person's Web page. Just follow these steps:

1. From the main Lycos Web page (www.lycos.com), select the Search Option link.

2. When the Pro Search page appears, enter the name of the person who owns the home page you're looking for in the Search For box.

3. In the Look For... section, check Personal Home Pages.

4. Click Go Get It to begin the search.

Lycos now displays a list of Tripod and GeoCities member pages that match your search criteria.

TIP

Lycos' Personal Homepage search only searches those home pages on the Tripod and GeoCities services. To learn more about Tripod, see Chapter 32, "Placing Personal Web Pages with Tripod and Angelfire."

ONCE YOU'VE FOUND THE PERSON YOU'RE LOOKING FOR...

Now that you've learned how to search for people on the Internet, it's time to take things a step further and look for *businesses* online. Just turn to Chapter 11, "Searching for Businesses," to learn more.

CHAPTER 11

SEARCHING FOR BUSINESSES

Many businesses today have a Web presence. Even businesses that don't have their own Web pages often are listed on other Web pages. It's easy to use Lycos and the Web to find information about businesses—from simple phone numbers to detailed company financials.

SEARCHING FOR BUSINESS WEB PAGES

If a business has its own Web page, chances are it's listed with Lycos. Just use the standard Lycos search (described in Chapter 9, "Searching the Web with Lycos") to search on the business' name; a list of all Web pages pertaining to that business name will be displayed.

SEARCHING FOR BUSINESS PHONE NUMBERS AND ADDRESSES

Whether or not a business has its own Web page, its basic business information—phone number and street address—will be listed in various "yellow pages" directories on the Internet. One of the best of these business directories is included, provided by GTE, and accessible from Lycos' main page.

You can use GTE's Yellow Pages to look for information on a specific business, or to list all businesses within a business category. To use GTE's Yellow Pages online, just follow these steps:

1. From the main Lycos Web page, click on the Yellow Pages link (or go directly to yp.gte.net).

2. When the GTE's Yellow Pages page appears (see Figure 11.1), enter either the business' Category or Business Name.

TIP

If you don't have a specific business in mind and you're not sure of the name of the particular business category, click the Top Categories link to display an alphabetical list of major Yellow Pages categories.

---

3. Now enter the City (if known) and State where the business resides.

4. Click the Find It button.

FIGURE 11.1
Use GTE's Yellow Pages to search for business phone numbers and addresses.

If prompted, choose from one of the categories listed;
GTE will display a list of businesses that match your
search criteria. Click on the specific business address to
display a map of that business' neighborhood.

TIP
....

If you know the business' phone number or the street where it's
located, enter that information for a more inclusive search. In
addition, you can click the Search by Distance link to search
for businesses within a specified radius of a given street
location.

SEARCHING FOR COMPANY
INFORMATION

If you're more interested in what a business does rather
than where it is, you can use Lycos to search for specific
company financial information. Lycos has partnered with
Dun & Bradstreet to offer the Companies Online service,
which lets you search for information about any public
and many private companies.

To use Companies Online, follow these steps:

1. From the main Lycos Web page, click on the
Companies Online link (or go directly to
www.companiesonline.com).

2. When the Companies Online page appears (see
Figure 11.2), either enter the company's name into
the Company Name box (along with as much other
information as you know), or enter the company's
stock symbol into the Ticker Symbol box. Click Go
Get It to proceed.

3. You will now be presented with a list of companies that match your search criteria. (Sometimes affiliates or branch offices will be included on this list.) Click on the company you wish to examine.

4. Basic information about the company—including D-U-N-S number, phone number, Web address(es), and general ownership information—will now be displayed.

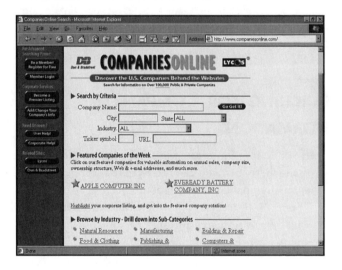

FIGURE 11.2
Use Companies Online to search for company financial information.

Additional resources are also available from this main company page. These resources can be free (stock quotes) or can carry a charge (for detailed business background reports). Just click on the resource you wish to view, and follow the directions on the following page.

FIND EVEN *MORE* COMPANY INFORMATION AT HOOVER'S ONLINE

Companies Online has a lot of good basic business information. But if you want even more detailed information about a particular company, you should check out Hoover's Online at www.hoovers.com. Hoover's is a site that specializes in providing detailed financial and operating information about publicly-traded corporations. For most public companies, you can find the following information:

➤ Company capsule (basic info)

➤ Company profile (history, operating info)

➤ Financials (basic, in-depth, and historical)

➤ Earnings estimates

➤ Comparative data with related companies

➤ Research analyst reports

➤ Annual reports and SEC filings

➤ News and press releases

You might have to click around a bit to find the specific information you're looking for—and you *will* have to pay for some of it—but if you're a serious investor, there's no better site to start with than Hoover's.

> **TIP**
>
> To learn more about finding financial information on the Web, turn to Chapter 18, "Managing Stocks and Finances Online."

ONCE YOU'VE FOUND THAT BUSINESS...

Now that you've learned about how to search the Internet for business information, it's time to get a little geeky. Turn to Chapter 12, "Searching for Files to Download," to learn how to find and download computer files from the Internet.

CHAPTER 12

SEARCHING FOR FILES TO DOWNLOAD

The Internet is a huge repository for computer files of all shapes and sizes, from utilities that help you better manage your disk drive to full-featured email and newsgroup programs. There are hundreds of thousands of these programs available *somewhere* on the Internet; if you can find them, you can download them to your computer.

Several big Web sites have been created to help users find various types of files. Among the most popular sites for file downloads are Macmillan's Tucows site at tucows.mcp.com and clnet's download.com site at www.download.com. In addition, Lycos has partnered with Ziff-Davis' ZDNet to offer access to the ZDNet Software Library, one of the largest collections of freeware and shareware programs on the Internet.

TIP

Many of these program files—called *freeware* programs—are available free of charge. Other programs can be downloaded for no charge, but require you to pay a token to receive full functionality or documentation; these are called *shareware* programs.

FINDING FILES WITH LYCOS

If you know the type of file you're looking for, the easiest thing to do is let Lycos do the searching for you. Just follow these steps:

1. From the Lycos main Web page, click the Free Software link.

2. When the Lycos Download Library page appears, enter the type of file you're looking for in the Search box. For example, if you're looking for a zip/unzip program, enter **zip**; if you're looking for a chat program, enter **chat**.

3. Click Go Get It. Lycos will now return a list of files from the ZDNet Software Library that match your search criteria. (See Figure 12.1.)

4. Click on the link to the file you wish to download. A full-page description of the file is displayed.

5. To download the file, click the Download Now button. When the File Download dialog box appears, select Save This File to Disk and click OK.

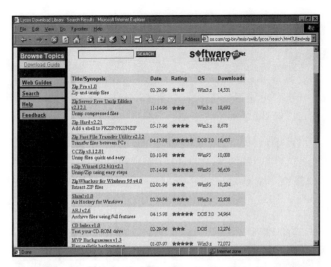

FIGURE 12.1
*A list of files from the ZDNet Software Library; each file is rated on a scale of
1 to 5 stars.*

After the file download is completed, install the file as
directed. (Installation instructions are usually included
somewhere on the ZDNet software page, or in a
"readme" file included with the file download.) In most
cases, installation involves running a file named setup.exe
or install.exe. To do this, click the Windows Start button,
select Run, and when the Run dialog box appears, type
the file path and name into the Open box and click OK.
Once the setup program launches, follow the onscreen
instructions to complete the installation.

TIP

Some files are downloaded in compressed zip format; before
you install these files, you'll need to first unzip the file. See the
Unzipping Files section later in this chapter for more details.

FINDING FILES ON ZDNET SOFTWARE LIBRARY

If you're not sure of which files you need, you can browse the ZDNet Software Library at www.hotfiles.com. Just follow these steps:

1. Go to the ZDNet Software Library main page at www.hotfiles.com (or www.zdnet.com/swlib).

2. Click on any of the software categories listed along the left side of the main page, as shown in Figure 12.2.

FIGURE 12.2
Browsing ZDNet's Software Library for files to download.

3. Navigate through the next few pages of subcategories, fine-tuning the types of files listed until you find the specific file you wish to download.

4. Once you find the file you wish to download, click on its link. A full-page description of the file is displayed.

5. To download the file, click the Download Now button. When the File Download dialog box appears, select Save This File to Disk and click OK.

Once the file is downloaded, follow the instructions for installing the file listed in the previous section.

TIP

All of the software libraries listed in this chapter are Web-based. You may also find repositories of files on the Internet that are *not* hosted on Web sites, but instead require the use of an *FTP* program for downloading. FTP (which stands for File Transfer Protocol) is an older technology still used by some sites; in some cases FTP downloads might be a tad faster than downloads from Web sites. Note that you don't have to have a separate FTP program to access FTP sites—you can use your Web browser as a quasi-FTP client! Just enter ftp:// plus the FTP site's address into your browser's address box, and the contents of the FTP site will appear in your browser window.

UNZIPPING FILES

Many program files are very large, and thus are *compressed* in some way to shorten downloading times. You may have to *decompress* a downloaded file before it can be installed; while some installation routines decompress files automatically, you may have to decompress some files manually.

The most popular compression system used over the Internet is called *zip*. Compressed files are said to be "zipped," and have a .zip extension. To decompress a zip file you "unzip" it.

There are many zip programs available for downloading from the ZDNet Software Library. The most popular is a program called WinZip; the Windows 95/98/NT version is available at the following Web page:

```
hotfiles.lycos.com/cgi-bin/texis/swlib/
lycos/info.html?fcode=000015.
```

Once WinZip is installed, you run the program to unzip compressed files, or zip selected files.

PROTECTING AGAINST VIRUSES

Computer viruses are programs that harm your computer in some fashion. Some are more annoying than harmful, but others can destroy the contents of your computer system and render it useless. You can protect yourself from viruses by being careful about what you put on your machine and running anti-virus software regularly.

Unfortunately, files on the Internet can be easily infected with viruses. The best prevention is to download files only from major download sites (such as the ZDNet Software Library), since unknown files from unknown sites pose the highest risk.

If you download files from the Internet, you should install an antivirus program on your computer. This program will check your system for viruses each time your system is booted. To be safe, you should download any programs from the Internet to a separate directory and scan them with the antivirus program before you run the new programs on your system.

You can find several popular antivirus programs at your local computer software retailer. My favorites are McAfee VirusScan (a free version of which is included with Microsoft Plus! 98) and Norton AntiVirus.

ONCE YOU'VE DOWNLOADED YOUR SOFTWARE...

Now that you've learned about how to find and download software from the Internet, it's time to have a little fun. Turn to Chapter 13, "Searching for Pictures, Sounds, and Movies," to learn how to find and download pictures and sounds from the Web.

CHAPTER 13

SEARCHING FOR PICTURES, SOUNDS, AND MOVIES

Computing doesn't have to be boring. You can make your PC more fun by adding pictures to your Windows desktop or documents, or by replacing your standard Windows sounds with other, off-the-wall sounds. Adding pictures or sounds to your system is easy—but where do you find new pictures and sounds?

The Internet is a treasure trove of picture, sound, and movie files. Pictures—also called *graphics*—are available in a variety of formats, as are sound and movie files. All you need is to know where to look, and then you can download all the pictures, sounds, and movies you want, direct from the Internet to your desktop.

UNDERSTANDING PICTURE, SOUND, AND MOVIE FILE FORMATS

There are numerous different kinds of picture and sound files. In addition, there are several different file formats for *moving* pictures, using full-motion video. These files are most commonly identified by their file extensions, and all have slightly different uses.

Table 13.1 explains some of the more common picture and sound file formats.

Table 13.1 Picture, Sound, and Movie File Formats

File Format	Description
.au	An audio format (standing for "audio") that originated on the Sun and NeXT computer systems.
.bmp	A simple graphics format (standing for "bitmap") that is the default format for Windows desktop backgrounds.
.gif	A popular Web-based graphics format (pronounced "jif"). GIF files can include transparent backgrounds (so a Web page background can show through) and can include multiple images for a simple animated effect.
.jpe	An alternate file extension for JPG graphics files.
.jpg	Another popular Web-based graphics format (pronounced "jay-peg"). JPG files are often slightly smaller in size than comparable GIF files.
.mid	An audio format (standing for "MIDI"—the **M**usical **I**nstrument **D**igital **I**nterface format used by professional musicians) used for longer music-based audio clips.
.mov	A video format (standing for "QuickTime Movie") used for video clips.
.mp3	An audio format that uses data compression to reduce digital sound files by a 12:1 ratio with virtually no loss in quality. The result is a high-quality, small file size version of a digital original; MP3 files are often used to make hard-disk copies of music from compact discs. (The file extension itself is short for **M**PEG Layer **3**, the technology behind the file format.)

File Format	Description
.mpg	A video format (pronounced "em-peg") used for video clips.
.pcx	An older graphics format (pronounced "pee-see-ex"), not normally used on Web pages. PCX files can be used as desktop backgrounds for more recent versions of Windows.
.pdf	A file type from Adobe that lets you view pages on your screen exactly as you'd see them on paper. (PDF stands for **P**age **D**efinition **F**ormat, by the way.)
.png	A newer graphics format (pronounced "ping") designed to ultimately replace the GIF format—although it's not yet widely used.
.qt	An alternate file extension for QuickTime Movie (.mov) files.
.ra	An audio format (standing for "RealAudio") designed for real-time streaming audio feeds.
.ram	A video format (standing for "RealMovie") designed for real-time streaming video feeds.
.rm	An alternate file extension for either RealAudio or RealMovie files.
.snd	An audio format (standing for "sound") similar to the AU format; not widely used on the Web.
.tif	A graphics format (pronounced "tif"), not widely used on Web pages. TIF files are popular with professional desktop publishers.
.wav	An audio format (pronounced "wave") used on many Web pages, as well as for Windows system sounds.

Now when you see a file with one of these file extensions, you'll know what kind of file it is and how you can use it.

USING LYCOS TO SEARCH FOR PICTURE AND MOVIE FILES

Lycos includes the PicturesNow! search engine that lets you search the Web for graphics and video files. In addition, Lycos provides access to the Now & Then Image Gallery, a collection of more than 40,000 images that are free of any usage charges.

TIP

Many image files on the Web are copyrighted, and cannot legally be used without payment for permission. While it's probably okay to download a graphics file for use on your personal computer (assuming the Feds aren't going to raid your house looking for illegal pictures), using Web graphics without permission for commercial use—for a newsletter or a personal Web page, for example—is definitely a legal no-no.

To use Lycos to search for picture files on the Web, follow these steps:

1. From the main Lycos Web page, click on the Pictures&Sounds link to display the Pictures & Sounds page. (See Figure 13.1.)
2. Select Search the Web for Pictures.
3. Enter a description of what you're looking for in the search box.
4. Click Go Get It.
5. When the list of results appears, click on the link to the picture or video file you wish to download.

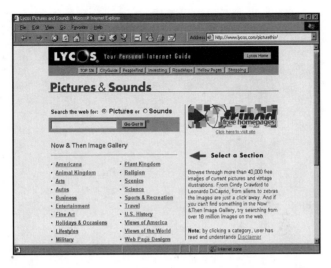

FIGURE 13.1
Searching the Web for pictures and sounds.

6. If you've clicked on a graphics file, the picture will now be displayed in your Web browser window, as shown in Figure 13.2. To save the file to your hard disk, right-click on the picture and select Save Picture As from the pop-up menu. When the Save Picture dialog box appears, select a folder for the picture file, then click Save.

7. If you've clicked on a movie file, your default video player will automatically launch and begin to play the video clip. If you want to save the file to your hard disk, you should go back to the page displayed in your Web browser, *right-click* on the link and select Save Target As from the pop-up menu. When the Save As dialog box appears, select a folder for the file, then click Save.

FIGURE 13.2
A picture of Yasmine Bleeth, ready for downloading—just right-click the picture and select Save Picture As.

TIP

You can also search for pictures and sounds directly form the Lycos main page at www.lycos.com. Just pull down the Search list, select either Pictures or Sounds, enter your search phrase in the For: box, then click the Go Get It button.

To search the Now & Then Image Gallery for pictures, follow these steps:

1. From the main Lycos Web page, click on the Pictures&Sounds link to display the Pictures & Sounds page.

2. Click on the desired category, then continue clicking within on subcategories until you find the image you're looking for.

3. Once the image you want is displayed, right-click on the picture and select Save Picture As from the pop-up menu.

4. When the Save Picture dialog box appears, select a folder for the picture file, then click <u>S</u>ave.

Once the picture file is saved to your hard disk, you can then insert it into various documents (including Word documents and HTML Web pages), or use Windows Control Panel to make the file your Windows desktop background.

USING LYCOS TO SEARCH FOR SOUND FILES

Searching for sound files is just like searching for picture files, except you have to be creative about how you describe the sound. For example, to display a list of scary door-opening sounds, enter **creaky door**.

Just follow these steps:

1. From the main Lycos Web page, click on the Pictures&Sounds link to display the Pictures & Sounds page.

2. Select Search the Web for Sounds.

3. Enter a description of the sound you're looking for in the search box.

4. Click Go Get It.

5. When the list of results appears, click on the link to the sound file you wish to download.

6. Windows will now display a File Download dialog box. Select Save This File to Disk and click OK.

7. When the Save As dialog box appears, select a folder for the file, then click <u>S</u>ave.

Once the sound file is saved to your hard disk, you can use various media players to play the sound. Just open My Computer or Windows Explorer, navigate to the folder that contains the sound file, and double-click on the file. The file should play automatically.

ONCE YOU'VE DOWNLOADED YOUR PICTURES AND SOUNDS...

Now that you've learned about how to find and download pictures, sounds, and movies from the Web, it's time to get a little more serious. See Chapter 14, "Reading the News, Weather, and Sports Online," to learn how to find news, weather, and other timely information on the Internet.

PART IV

SHOPPING AND OTHER FUN ACTIVITIES

CHAPTER 14

READING THE NEWS, WEATHER, AND SPORTS ONLINE

You can get just about all the news you want on the World Wide Web—current news headlines, in-depth topic analyses, specialized industry and company news, even news customized for your city or town. In fact, almost every major newspaper, magazine, and television news organization has a site on the Web, many of which offer more current news than you'll find in their old-media versions.

One good thing about getting news, sports, and weather information online is that it's always up-to-date. Most news-based Web sites update their information constantly, so you can find out what's happening pretty much as it happens. You don't have to wait around for the nightly news report, the morning newspaper, or the weekly newsmagazine.

THE BEST GENERAL NEWS SITES ON THE WEB

Lycos has its own news site, accessible from the News link on the main Lycos Web page, that displays the latest news headlines. You can also go directly to www.lycos.com/news, a page that displays a wider variety of headlines in various categories.

Many dedicated news organizations, however, offer more complete news sites. The most popular of these full-featured news sites are run by the major cable networks and national newspapers, and include:

➤ **CNN Interactive** (www.cnn.com—see Figure 14.1)

➤ **FOX News** (www.foxnews.com)

➤ **MSNBC** (www.msnbc.com)

➤ **New York Times** (www.nytimes.com)

➤ **USA Today** (www.usatoday.com)

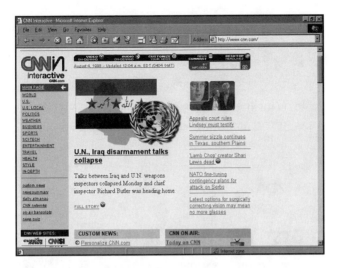

FIGURE 14.1
Catch all the news from CNN's Web site at www.cnn.com.

TIP

On the CNN site, click the Custom News link to create a custom-made page of news stories personalized to your tastes.

THE BEST SPECIALIZED NEWS SITES ON THE WEB

In addition to the general news sites, there are numerous Web sites that provide specialized news reporting. For example, c|net (www.cnet.com) is a great site for computer industry news. Here is a handful of other specialized news sites on the Web:

➤ **Ain't It Cool News** insider entertainment news
(www.aint-it-cool-news.com)

> ➤ **c|net** computer news (www.cnet.com)
> ➤ **CNNfn** financial news (www.cnnfn.com)
> ➤ **Mr. Showbiz** entertainment news (www.mrshowbiz.com)
> ➤ **Quicken.com** financial news (www.quicken.com)
> ➤ **TV Guide Entertainment Network** television news (www.tvguide.com)
> ➤ **Ultimate TV** television news (www.ultimatetv.com)
> ➤ **ZDNet** computer news (www.zdnet.com)

THE BEST WEATHER SITES ON THE WEB

There are many weather-related resources on the Web. Lycos has its own weather site, accessible from the Weather link on the main Lycos Web page (or directly at weather.lycos.com). The Lycos weather site provides a variety of forecasts and weather maps, including local forecasts for specific zip codes.

The most popular weather site on the Web, however, is **The Weather Channel** at www.weather.com. This site (see Figure 14.2) includes the largest variety of forecasts and maps, including travel forecasts and conditions for most major U.S. airports (just click the Travel Wise link).

TIP
....
To customize the main Weather Channel page with your hand-picked maps and city forecasts, click the Customize Your Home Page link and follow the on-screen instructions.

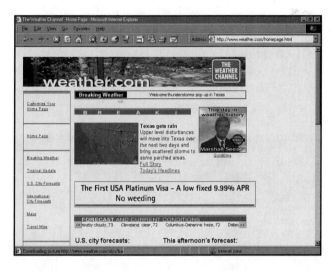

FIGURE 14.3
*Every kind of weather forecast you can think of is available on The Weather
Channel's site at www.weather.com.*

If you don't like The Weather Channel's site, there are
several other popular weather sites on the Web, including:

➤ **AccuWeather** (www.accuweather.com)

➤ **INTELLiCast** (www.intellicast.com)

➤ **National Weather Service** (www.nws.noaa.gov)

➤ **USA Today Weather**
(www.usatoday.com/weather/wfront.htm)

➤ **Weather Planner** (www.weatherplanner.com)

THE BEST SPORTS SITES ON THE WEB

The most popular sports site on the Web belongs to the
ESPN cable sports network. The **ESPN SportsZone** at
espn.sportszone.com (see Figure 14.4) includes all the
scores and in-depth reporting you expect from ESPN.

FIGURE 14.4
Check the latest scores and sports news from ESPN SportsZone at
espn.sportszone.com.

TIP

To create an up-to-the-minute sports score ticker on your desktop, click on the Real-Time ScoreTracker link on the ESPN
main page.

Other popular sports sites include:

➤ **CBS SportsLine** (www.sportsline.com)

➤ **Major League Baseball**
   (www.majorleaguebaseball.com)

➤ **NBA.com** (www.nba.com)

➤ **NBC Sports** (www.nbcsports.com)

➤ **National Football League** (www.nfl.com)

➤ **XPC Sports** (www.xpcsports.com)

There are also many fan-created Web sites for specific
sports and activities. Just go to Lycos' Sports community
page (www.lycos.com/sports) and search for your favorite
sport!

ONCE YOU HAVE YOUR FILL OF NEWS...

Now that you've learned about the best sites for national
news, weather, and sports, it's time to find some local
information on the Web. Turn to Chapter 15, "Getting
Local Information Online," to learn how to locate local
information online.

CHAPTER 15

GETTING LOCAL INFORMATION ONLINE

While the World Wide Web contains millions of sites from around the world (hence its name), there are times when you want information about places and events closer to home. Fortunately, there is a new breed of so-called local Web sites, where locals can search for nearby businesses, and travelers can find out all about their destinations without leaving home.

One of the best collections of local sites is City Guide, from Lycos (`cityguide.lycos.com`). City Guide includes local pages for hundreds of cities around the world—and each local page includes local news, sports scores, weather reports, tourist info, road maps, and a variety of other region-specific information.

EXPLORING LYCOS CITY GUIDE

While each City Guide is unique (based on the information available for a given city), let's take a look at a sample City Guide to see what you'll find.

First, you need to locate the City Guide page for the city you're interested in; just follow these steps:

1. From the main Lycos Web page, click on the City Guide link (or go directly to cityguide.lycos.com).

2. When the next page appears, either click on a region of the map or select a country from the pull-down list, enter the name of the desired city, and click Go Get It.

3. Use the next page (or pages, if you're using the map) to select the specific city you wish to explore.

4. The City Guide for your desired city, shown in Figure 15.1, contains a short background article about that city—as well as a variety of other information.

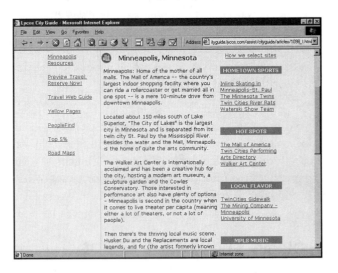

FIGURE 15.1
Learn all about a specific city with Lycos City Guide.

Once you've brought up the local City Guide page, you can click on the appropriate links to find the following information:

➤ Read about the hottest local destinations by clicking on a link in the **Hot Spots** section.

➤ Look for local music and entertainment under the **Music** section.

➤ Explore other local attractions and events by clicking a link in the **Local Flavor** section.

➤ Check in on the local sports teams by selecting a link in the **Hometown Sports** section.

➤ Read the local news by clicking a link under the **News Links** heading.

➤ Find out key local information—population, school districts, and so on—in the **Vital Stats** section.

➤ Look at pictures from the selected city by clicking one of the links in the **Visual Relief** section.

ACCESSING LYCOS'S CITY RESOURCE PAGES

In addition to local City Guide pages, Lycos also offers special city resource pages for many cities. Access this page for a given city by clicking the Resources link on the local City Guide page.

As you can see in Figure 15.2, the following information is located on a typical city resource page:

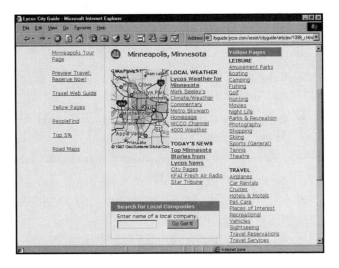

FIGURE 15.2
Access even more city information from Lycos' City Resource Page.

➤ Zoom in on the local area by clicking anywhere on the local city map—or display a detailed map of a specific location by entering street address in the **Get Local Map** box and clicking Go Get It.

➤ Search for local businesses by clicking one of the business category links in the **Yellow Pages** section, or by entering a business name or category in the **Search for Local Companies** box and clicking Go Get It.

➤ Search for the street addresses and phone numbers of local residents by entering first and/or last name information in the **Search For Local People** box and clicking Go Get It.

➤ Read local news by clicking a link in the **Today's News** section.

➤ Find out the local forecast by clicking any link under the **Local Weather** heading.

Other Local Web Sites

If you can't find what you're looking for with Lycos City Guide, there are numerous other local guides available on the Web. While many of these sites are specific to a single city, there are also several networks of local sites, including:

➤ **CitySearch** (www.citysearch.com)

➤ **DigitalCity** (www.digitalcity.com)

➤ **Microsoft Sidewalk** (www.sidewalk.com)

➤ **USA CityLink** (usacitylink.com)

Whether you're a local or a tourist, you should find any of these local Web sites quite useful!

Once You've Seen the Local Sites...

Now that you've learned how to find local information on the Web, it's time to think about getting out of town for awhile. Turn to Chapter 16, "Planning a Trip Online," to learn how to plan your next trip using the Internet.

CHAPTER 16

PLANNING A TRIP ONLINE

In the "old days" (pre-Web, pre-1994) if you wanted to travel, you called a travel agent. You had to trust the travel agent to find the lowest fares, the most direct flights, the best accommodations, and the most appropriate excursions—in other words, you put your hard-earned vacation in the hands of a stranger, and hoped that person knew what you wanted and could cut you the best deals available.

Today, it's a different world. While you can still use a travel agent (and often have to pay for the privilege), it's now just as easy to plan your vacations using the Internet, from the comfort of your own home, using your own keyboard and mouse. In fact, many Internet users discover that they find *better* accommodations, reservations, and travel information online—and save a few bucks, besides!

SEARCH FOR TRAVEL-RELATED RESOURCES

The World Wide Web offers a wealth of travel resources. Here are just a few places to start—beginning with Lycos' many travel-related offerings:

➤ Go to Lycos main travel site at www.lycos.com/travel (see Figure 16.1). (You can also get there by clicking the Travel link on the main Lycos page.) From here you can get information about specific destinations, read the latest travel news, access specific travel community guides, and link to other travel resources on the Web.

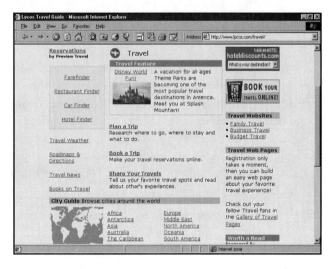

FIGURE 16.1
Start planning your vacation at Lycos Travel community site
(www.lycos.com/travel).

➤ Use the Lycos Book a Trip page (www.lycos.com/travel/bookatrip.html/) to access a variety of commercial travel providers.

➤ Access Lycos' City Guide (cityguide.lycos.com) to get detailed information about specific cities.

➤ Find out the weather forecast and travel conditions—including the latest airport conditions—from Lycos Travel Weather page (weather.lycos.com/travel.asp).

➤ Discover the best travel deals at Arthur Frommer's Outspoken Encyclopedia of Travel (www.frommers.com).

MAKE YOUR RESERVATIONS

Once you've researched *where* you want to go, it's time to make your reservations. There are a number of sites on the Web that let you book flight, hotel, and rental car reservations; you can access several of these sites directly from the Lycos Book a Trip site (www.lycos.com/travel/bookatrip.html/).

Lycos' preferred travel provider is **Preview Travel**. You can access this online travel agency by clicking the Reservations link on the Book a Trip page, or by going directly to previewtravel.lycos.com (see Figure 16.2). Once you access Preview Travel, click Destination Guides to learn more about a specific destination; click Travel Reservations to make air, hotel, and car reservations; click Farefinder to search for the best airfares; or click Carfinder to search for the best auto rental rates.

T I P

Preview Travel, like many online travel sites, requires that you become a "member" before you can access their complete list of services. Not to worry—becoming a member doesn't cost you anything, and you get the added benefit of the site remembering your travel preferences on any subsequent visit.

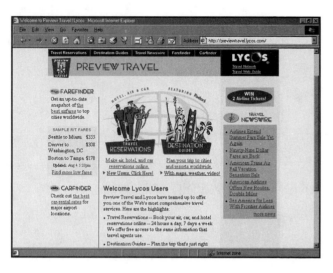

Figure 16.2
Use Preview Travel (previewtravel.lycos.com) to find the best fares and make your reservations.

Preview Travel is just one of many places on the Web where you can search for low fares and make all your travel reservations—and all these sites work pretty much the same way, with similar databases of information. Here is a short list of some of the other popular travel reservation sites:

➤ **Internet Travel Network** (www.itn.net)

➤ **Microsoft Expedia** (www.expedia.com)

➤ **TravelNow** (www.travelnow.com)

➤ **Travelocity** (www.travelocity.com)

➤ **Travelon** (www.travelon.com)

➤ **TravelWeb** (www.travelweb.com)

Whichever site you choose to use, you'll need to know *when* you're traveling (your departure and return dates), *how many* people are traveling, *how much* you want to pay (full fare or discount fare), *what kind* of arrangements and accommodations you want, and any *special considerations* you have for your trip. Armed with this information (and your credit card number!), you can make your reservations right from your keyboard.

GET DIRECTIONS—AND DRAW A MAP!

Once you've made all your reservations, it's a good idea to get a map of where you're going—or, if you're driving, directions on how to get there. There are all sorts of mapping services available on the Internet, and one of the best is available from Lycos.

Here's how to use Lycos to create a map of your vacation destination:

1. Access Lycos' Road Maps by clicking the Road Maps link on the main Lycos Web page, or go directly to www.lycos.com/roadmap.html.

2. To draw a specific map, enter as much of the following information as you know: street address or intersection, city, state, zip code, and country. Click Go Get It to display the map (see Figure 16.3).

TIP

Once the map is displayed, select a different Zoom Level to display more or less of the selected region. To center the map around a different spot, make sure Center is selected and click on the new center point. You can also pan the map in a specific direction by clicking on one of the directional coordinates (NE, E, SE, etc.).

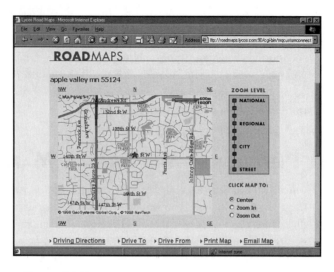

FIGURE 16.3
The Lycos Road Maps takes you where you need to go.

3. To calculate directions from one location to another, click the Driving Directions link. When the next page appears, enter your starting point and ending point, and select which type of directions you'd like to display. (You can select text-only directions, text with one big map, or text with individual maps for each turn or change in direction.) Click the Calculate Directions button to display the directions.

Now, with research done, reservations made, and map and directions in hand, you're finally ready to leave on that vacation—which is the one thing you *can't* do from the comfort of your keyboard!

> **TIP**
>
> If you really like maps, take a look at Microsoft's TerraServer site (www.terraserver.microsoft.com), which serves up finely detailed aerial maps taken from orbiting satellites!

ONCE YOU'VE RETURNED FROM YOUR TRIP...

Now that you've learned about how to find travel information and book reservations online, it's time to kick back and do a little shopping. Turn to Chapter 17, "Going Shopping Online," to learn how to shop and order merchandise from the Internet.

CHAPTER 17

GOING SHOPPING ONLINE

Shopping online is easier than shopping in the real world. You can sit in front of your computer at any time of day or night, dressed or undressed, and use your keyboard to search the Internet for just the right item you want to buy—you don't have to get dressed up or start up your car or bother with boisterous crowds. To purchase an item online, all you have to do is enter your name, address, and credit card number, and the online merchant will arrange to have the item delivered directly to your house within a matter of days. It's that easy!

In fact, shopping online is just like shopping from a catalog, with the added benefit of being able to access all the merchants in a given category with the click of your mouse. It's also a safe way to shop; most online merchants use "secure" servers (in combination with the "secure" modes built into Internet Explorer and Netscape Navigator), so giving your credit card number online is just as safe as giving it to a catalog merchant over the phone.

SHOPPING FOR ONLINE SHOPS

Lycos offers access to a large number of online stores offering a wide variety of goods and services, from apparel to wine. To find the online retailer you want, follow these steps:

1. Access the Lycos Shopping Network (see Figure 17.1) by clicking the Shopping link on the main Lycos Web page, or by going directly to www.lycos.com/shopnet.

FIGURE 17.1
Use the Lycos Shopping Network to search for a wide variety of online merchants.

2. To search for a merchant by business category, click on one of the category links on the **Categories** section on the left side of the page.

3. To compare prices on similar items from multiple online stores, click the Compare Prices link.

Once you find the merchant you want, follow that merchant's online instructions to find and buy specific merchandise online.

SHOPPING FOR BOOKS

More online shoppers buy books than any other type of merchandise. Shopping for books online is fast and easy, and you can find just about any title you can think of—there are more books available in online "bookstores" than there are in any physical bookstore.

Barnes and Noble is the world's largest physical bookseller, and Barnesandnoble.com (www.barnesandnoble.com) is one of the largest bookstores on the Internet. Lycos has partnered with Barnes and Noble to bring users the best bargains on the most books online.

To find a particular book on Barnes and Noble's online site, just follow these directions:

1. Go to Lycos' link to Barnesandnoble.com by clicking the Barnes & Noble link on the main Lycos Web page, or by going directly to http://www.lycos.com/ shopnet/books (see Figure 17.2).

2. To search for a book by title, pull down the Search For list and select Title, then enter all or part of the title in the search box, and click Go Get It.

3. To search for a book by author's name, pull down the Search For list and select Author, then enter all or part of the author's name in the search box, and click Go Get It.

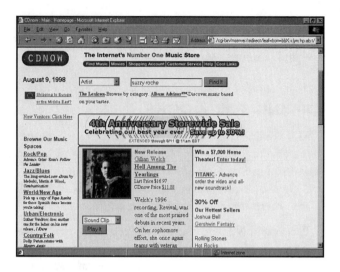

FIGURE 17.2
*Use Lycos to access one of the biggest bookstores on the Internet,
Barnesandnoble.com.*

4. To search for a book by subject or other criteria (such
as "mystery"), pull down the Search For list and
select Keyword, then enter one or more words in the
search box, and click Go Get It.

5. To look at recommended books in a given subject
area, click the subject area link in the Subjects area.

6. To view details about a particular book, click on the
title for the book you want; when the main book page
appears, click Add To My Cart to order the book.
Click Continue Shopping to look for more books;
click Continue Checkout to finish shopping and place
your order.

7. When you're ready to "check out" and complete your
order, click the View Shoppping Cart link.

8. The next page will list all the books in your current shopping cart; click `Continue Checkout` to continue, and follow the onscreen instructions.

Here are some tips for using Barnesandnoble.com:

➤ If you want to search using more detailed criteria than just title, author, or keyword (such as the book's ISBN number), click the `Search` link on any page *except* the front page and use the Search Books page that appears.

➤ If you're viewing an individual book page, you can look for similar books by scrolling down to the bottom of the page and selecting one or more keywords, then clicking Go.

➤ To find other books by the author of a specific book, click the author's name on the individual book page.

➤ To order just one book quickly, click the `Express Lane` link on any book page and follow the on-screen directions.

➤ Barnesandnoble.com also sells computer software; click the `Software Home` link (visible on every page *except* the home page) to access their online software store.

➤ To look for more books from this author, do an author search for either Michael Miller or Mike Miller! (Tip: There are several authors who share my name; if it's not a computer book—or *Webster's New World Vocabulary of Success*—I probably didn't write it!)

TIP

Barnes & Noble's Web site is just one of several online book-sellers. Other popular Internet bookstores include Amazon.com (www.amazon.com), Borders.com (www.borders.com), and Books.com (www.books.com).

SHOPPING FOR MUSIC

Just as Lycos has partnered with Barnes and Noble to offer users a great selection of books online, Lycos has also part-nered with one of the largest online music stores to offer users a great selection of CDs and tapes online. CDnow (www.cdnow.com) is one of the Internet's largest retailers of compact discs, audio cassettes, and videocassettes. Not only can you buy music online at CDnow, you can also *sample* music online via downloadable music clips from many albums.

To find a particular CD on CDnow, just follow these directions:

1. Go to Lycos' link to CDnow by clicking the CDnow link on the main Lycos Web page, or by going directly to www.cdnow.com (see Figure 17.3).

2. To search for all releases by a particular artist, select Artist from the pull-down list, enter all or part of the artist's name in the search box, then click Find It. When the artist's page appears, click on the price next to the format to order that particular release.

3. To search for a particular CD release, select Title from the pull-down list, enter all or part of the album title, then click Find It. Select the release you want from the results listed; when the CD's page appears, click on the price next to the format to order that particular release.

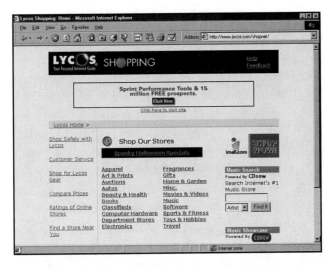

FIGURE 17.3
CDnow has a huge selection of music for sale; search by artist to find all releases from that artist.

4. To search a CD that contains a specific song, select Song Title from the pull-down list, enter all or part of the song's title in the search box, then click Find It. Select the release you want from the results listed; when the CD's page appears, click on the price next to the format to order that particular release.

5. To search for all releases on a specific record label, select label from the pull-down list, enter all or part of the label's name in the search box, then click Find It. Select the release you want from the results listed; when the CD's page appears, click on the price next to the format to order that particular release.

6. To search for a specific movie or musical soundtrack, select Soundtrack from the pull-down list, enter all or part of the movie or play's name in the search box, then click Find It. Select the release you want from the results listed; when the CD's page appears, click on the price next to the format to order that particular release.

7. To look at recommended releases in a given music genre, click the subject area link in the Browse Our Music Spaces. Once in that area, click on an individual release title to see the page for that CD; when the CD's page appears, click on the price next to the format to order that particular release.

8. When you're ready to "check out" and complete your order, click the Shopping Account link.

9. The next page will list all the selections in your current shopping cart; click Proceed to Checkout to continue, and follow the on-screen instructions.

Here are some tips for using CDnow:

➤ To find out what related artists CDnow recommends, click the Album Advisor link on the artist's page.

➤ To read a detailed article about an artist, click the Biography link on the artist's page.

➤ To see a list of other Web sites devoted to that artist, click the Web Links link on the artist's page.

➤ To read a review of a particular album, click the REVIEW link next to a release on the artist's page.

➤ To listen to an audio clip from a particular album, click the "music note" link next to a release on the artist's page.

➤ CDnow also offers movies for sale, on videotape, videodisc, and DVD. Click the Movies link on CDnow's home page to access their online movie store.

TIP

CDnow is just one of several online music retailers. Other popular music sites include Music Boulevard (www.musicblvd.com), Amazon.com (www.amazon.com), and Tunes.com (www.tunes.com).

SHOPPING FOR CARS ONLINE

It makes sense that books and compact discs are popular online purchases—they're small and easily shipped, and you don't have to "try them on" before you buy them. Buying an automobile online, though, seems like a different proposition.

You'd be surprised to see how many people are using the Internet to help them shop for new cars. While you can't get a brand new 1999 Corvette shipped to your doorstep via UPS, you can find a wealth of information about new cars online, including dealer cost information that can help you negotiate a better purchase price.

If you're in the mood for a new car, here are some sites to check out:

➤ **Auto-By-Tel** (www.autobytel.com), the granddaddy of Internet car sites. Auto-By-Tel is unique in that it helps match you up with dealers in your area who offer special discount prices.

➤ **AutoSite** (www.autosite.com), a comprehensive new car information site. Includes side-by-side comparisons and a special loan/lease calculator.

➤ **Cars.com** (www.cars.com), a comprehensive site for information about both new and used cars. This site includes used car classifieds, and is the home site for the popular NPR show, "Car Talk."

➤ **Edmund's Automobile Buyer's Guide** (www.edmunds.com), from the makers of the popular new car price guides. All the lowdown on prices and dealer incentives, for both new and used cars.

➤ **Kelley Blue Book** (www.kbb.com), from the publisher of the famous "blue book" price guides, pricing information for thousands of new and used car models.

➤ **Microsoft CarPoint** (carpoint.msn.com), my personal favorite auto site, complete with lots of new car comparisons and unique "surround video" tours of many models.

ONCE YOU'VE SHOPPED 'TIL YOU'VE DROPPED...

Now that you've learned how to spend lots of money at online retailers, it's time practice a little fiscal frugality. Turn to Chapter 18, "Managing Stocks and Finances Online," to learn how to manage your stocks and personal finances online.

CHAPTER 18

MANAGING STOCKS AND
FINANCES ONLINE

In the old days (pre-Web), if you wanted financial advice, you had to pay a financial advisor. Today, however, you can use a variety of online resources to research financial options, track stock performance, and even buy and sell stocks and other securities. And, unlike the old days, most of these financial resources are *free*.

Even with all these free financial resources, however, you still might want to invest in professional, personalized financial advice. Given the old saying that a fool and his money are soon parted, remember that the Internet lets you part with your money even more quickly than you could in the old, pre-Web days!

USING LYCOS'S INVESTING PAGE

Lycos offers a full-featured Investing page for Internet-based investors; just click the Stocks link on the main Lycos Web page, or go directly to investing.lycos.com. As you can see in Figure 18.1, Lycos's Investing page offers you a variety of features, including:

➤ On the `Front Page`, find the latest market headlines, search for specific stock quotes, and get a snapshot of your own personal portfolio.

➤ On the `News` page, find a variety of market and financial news stories.

➤ On the `Funds` page, find in-depth financial analysis on a variety of mutual funds.

➤ On the `Portfolio` page, get a detailed look at your own personal portfolio. (See the next section for details on how to manage your Lycos portfolio.)

➤ On the `Trading` page, gain access to a variety of online brokerages.

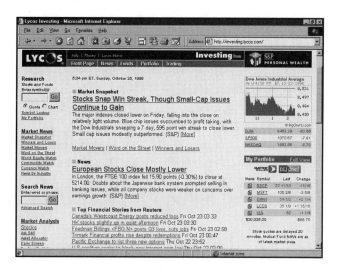

FIGURE 18.1

Use Lycos's Investing page to help you manage your personal financial investments.

TIP

Click the Money link at the top of any page to access Lycos's Money community, with links to a variety of finance-related Web sites.

CREATING AND MONITORING A STOCK PORTFOLIO

Lycos lets you create your own online securities portfolio, which you can monitor and manage directly from the Lycos Investing site. Follow these steps to set up the securities in your personal portfolio:

1. From the main Investing page (investing.lycos.com), click the Portfolio link.

2. When the Portfolio page appears (see Figure 18.2), click the Edit link.

3. When the Edit Portfolio page appears, enter the Symbol, Quantity of shares, Price per share, and Date of acquisition into the blanks for each security you wish to monitor. Click the Submit button when finished.

4. Your new portfolio is now displayed. To change the view of your portfolio, pull down the View list, select a new option, then click Go Get It.

5. To view more detailed information about an individual security, click the Symbol link in the Portfolio list.

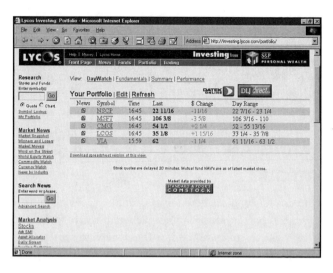

FIGURE 18.2
Monitor your own portfolio of securities on the Lycos Investing site.

OTHER FINANCIAL SITES ON THE WEB

Lycos's Investing site is just one of many finance-oriented sites on the Web. Here is a list of just a few of the more popular investing and personal finance sites:

➤ **Bank Rate Monitor** (www.bankrate.com), presents a variety of up-to-date loan, mortgage, and other rates.

➤ **BigCharts** (www.bigcharts.com), a great financial resource, filled with numerous charts and reports.

➤ **CNNfn** (cnnfn.com), the online home of the CNN Financial News network.

➤ **Companies Online** (www.companiesonline.com), a partnership between Dun & Bradstreet and Lycos, where you can find information on hundreds of thousands of public and private companies.

➤ **Homebuyer's Fair** (www.homefair.com), a great site for anyone thinking of buying or selling a home.

➤ **Hoovers Online** (www.hoovers.com), *the* place to research detailed financial information on public companies.

➤ **Invest-O-Rama** (www.investorama.com), a comprehensive directory of online investment resources.

➤ **Microsoft HomeAdvisor** (homeadvisor.msn.com), Microsoft's site for home buyers and sellers.

➤ **Microsoft Investor** (investor.msn.com), Microsoft's full-service site for online investors.

➤ **The Motley Fool** (www.fool.com), my personal favorite financial site, chock-full of useful information and analysis—one of the most truly useful sites on the Web for the personal investor.

➤ **Quicken.com** (www.quicken.com), a comprehensive personal finance site from the company that brings you Quicken software.

➤ **QuoteCom** (www.quote.com), a comprehensive personal finance and investing site.

➤ **Realtor.com** (www.realtor.com), the official site of the National Association of Realtors, filled with over a million listings for new and resale homes.

Using Online Stock Brokers

Not only can you monitor stock performance and research stocks on the Web, you can also buy and sell securities through a variety of online stock brokers—right from your personal computer. Lycos's preferred brokerage is **DLJ Direct** (www.dljdirect.com), although there are dozens of online brokerages competing for your business today. Here are a few of the larger online brokerages:

➤ **Accutrade** (www.accutrade.com)

➤ **American Express**
  (www.americanexpress.com/direct)

➤ **Charles Schwab** (www.schwab.com)

➤ **Discover Brokerage** (www.discoverbrokerage.com)

➤ **DLJ Direct** (www.dljdirect.com—see Figure 18.3)

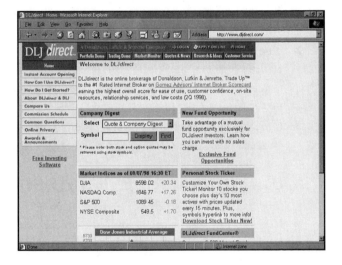

FIGURE 18.3
Buy and sell stocks online at DLJ Direct (www.dljdirect.com).

➤ **E*TRADE** (www.etrade.com)

➤ **Fidelity** (www.fidelity.com)

➤ **InvesTrade** (www.investrade.com)

➤ **Quick & Reilly** (www.quick-reilly.com)

➤ **SURETRADE** (www.suretrade.com)

TIP

The price per trade varies significantly from one online brokerage to another. Do your research before you sign up with a specific brokerage firm; make sure you get the right balance of price and performance (in the form of additional services) for your own personal needs.

ONCE YOU'VE MADE A BUNDLE ON THE MARKET...

Now that you've learned how to manage your finances and play the stock market online, it's time to close your checkbook and get back to work! Turn to Chapter 19, "Finding a Job Online," to learn how to do your job hunting online.

CHAPTER 19

FINDING A JOB ONLINE

Finding a job has never been easier, now that many employers are using the Web as a key recruiting device. You can find job postings from hundreds of thousands of firms with just a few keystrokes, and sort through the jobs you want based on the criteria you select.

For that matter, you can let the Web do the searching for you. Leave your online résumé at one or more of these career-oriented sites, and potential employers will be sending *you* email about positions they have open that match your qualifications.

TIP

In addition to the career-oriented Web sites discussed in this chapter, you can also find positions posted on many USENET newsgroups. Look for job postings in vocation-specific newsgroups, or in special ***.jobs** newsgroups. (These are generally region-specific listings; for example, you would find jobs in Minnesota listed in the **mn.jobs** newsgroup.)

To learn more about USENET newsgroups, see Part VI, "Communicating in Newsgroups."

Using Lycos's Career Resources

Lycos offers a variety of career-oriented resources to help
you manage your career and find your next job. These
resources include:

➤ **Lycos Careers community** (click the Careers link
on the main Lycos Web page, or go directly to
www.lycos.com/careers). Includes links to a variety
of career-related resources. (See Figure 19.1.)

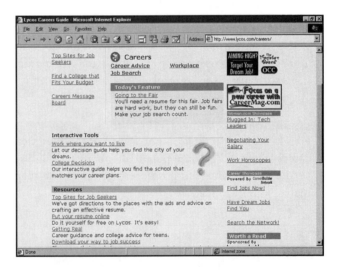

FIGURE 19.1
Use Lycos's Careers community as a starting point to your online job search.

➤ **Lycos Career Guide**
(www.lycos.com/careers/careerguide), simple links
to online job finders, self-employment, résumé
builders, and other resources.

➤ **Lycos Career Advice** (www.lycos.com/wguide/ network/net_484429.html), a listing of resources that can help you with your career planning.

➤ **Lycos Job Search** (www.lycos.com/wguide/ network/net_484430.html), a listing of job-related sites by profession.

THE BEST CAREER-ORIENTED SITES ON THE WEB

There are dozens of sites on the Web where you can look for jobs—or have employers look for you, when you post your online résumé. Many of these sites let you post your résumés at no charge; most charge employers to place ads or when positions are filled. Here are some of the more popular online job sites:

➤ **4work** (www.4work.com), an easy-to-use search engine that lets you search for jobs by state and keyword.

➤ **CareerBuilder Network** (www.careerbuilder.com), an all-purpose job-hunting site for both job-seekers and employers.

➤ **CareerMosaic** (www.careermosaic.com), one of the oldest and largest full-service career sites, with a variety of career-related resources, as well as standard job-wanted services.

➤ **CareerPath** (www.careerpath.com), one of the largest job-hunting sites on the Web, with listings from most major newspapers.

➤ **CareerSite** (www.careersite.com), an all-purpose job-hunting site, complete with "virtual agents" and "virtual recruiters" to match employers and potential employees.

➤ **E.Span** (www.espan.com), one of the oldest job-hunting sites on the Web, for both job-seekers and employers.

➤ **Futurestep** (www.futurestep.com), a newer career-oriented site, run by the *Wall Street Journal*, focusing on executive-level positions.

➤ **HeadHunter.NET** (www.headhunter.net), an all-purpose site specializing in middle and upper management positions.

➤ **HEART Career.com** (www.career.com), an all-purpose job-hunting site for both job-seekers and employers.

➤ **Hot Jobs** (www.hotjobs.com), a great site for technical and computer-oriented positions.

➤ **jobfind.com** (www.jobfind.com), a full-service career-oriented site, with job listings, career news, and corporate profiles.

➤ **JobTrak** (www.jobtrak.com), a job-listing service with special features designed specifically for college students and alumni.

➤ **JobWeb** (www.jobweb.com), a student-oriented career site from the National Association of Colleges and Employers.

➤ **Monster Board** (www.monster.com), one of the Web's largest sites for job listings. (See Figure 19.2.)

➤ **NationJob** (www.nationjob.com), an all-purpose job-hunting site for both job seekers and employers.

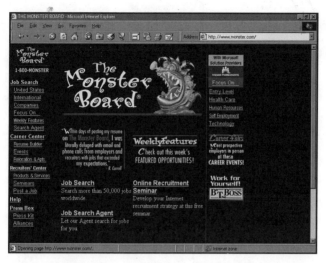

FIGURE 19.2

The Monster Board (www.monster.com), one of the many sites where you can find a job online.

➤ **Online Career Center** (www.occ.com), job listings and career-oriented news.

➤ **Recruiters Online Network** (ipa.com), a site that compiles services from more than 20,000 recruiting firms.

> **T I P**
>
> If you want to be absolutely, positively sure that your current employer can't trace a job-wanted ad back to you, *don't* use your work email address, and *don't* use your normal email address. Instead, create a new email address (under an untraceable name) using one of the many Web-based email services, such as Hotmail (www.hotmail.com) or LycosMail (email.lycos.com, explained in Chapter 23, "Using LycosMail").

ONCE YOU'VE NEGOTIATED A BIG SIGNING BONUS...

Now that you've learned how to find a job online, it's time to learn about other types of online classified advertising. Turn to Chapter 20, "Placing and Responding to Classified Ads Online," to learn how to place and respond to classified ads online.

CHAPTER 20

PLACING AND RESPONDING TO CLASSIFIED ADS ONLINE

You can buy and sell just about anything over the Internet. In fact, it's easier to search for items via online classified ads than it is in traditional newspaper classifieds—all you have to do is input what you're looking for, and the Lycos search engine finds it for you!

There are many classified ads sites on the Web, but Lycos has partnered with the Classifieds2000 service to offer you the most and the best classifieds. Through Lycos you can find classified ads in a variety of categories, including computers, general merchandise, jobs, real estate, rentals and roommates, and vehicles. Lycos even has online personal ad listings.

SEARCHING LYCOS CLASSIFIED ADS

It's easy to search Lycos' classified ads. Just follow these steps:

1. Go to the main Lycos Classifieds page (see Figure 20.1) by clicking the Classifieds link on the main Lycos Web page, or directly at www.lycos.com/shopnet/classifieds.

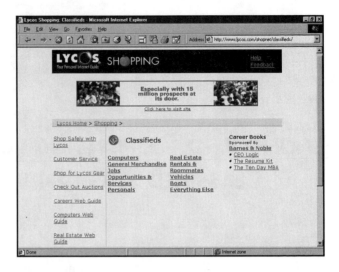

FIGURE 20.1
Use Lycos Classifieds to search for items for sale from private individuals.

2. Select the category you wish to search.

3. When the Search Ads page appears, select a specific subcategory.

4. When the next page appears, select your specific Area, as well as other search criteria, then click the Search button.

5. When the search results are displayed, click an individual ad header to display the entire ad.

6. To communicate with that particular seller, click the Send Message button and follow the onscreen instructions to compose and send an email message.

Once you've communicated with a seller, it's up to you to negotiate a price and close the sale. And you can do it all via email!

PLACING A CLASSIFIED AD

Lycos also lets you place your own classified ads. Just follow these steps:

1. Go to the main Lycos Classifieds page (see Figure 20.1) by clicking the Classifieds link on the main Lycos Web page, or directly at www.lycos.com/shopnet/classifieds.

2. You'll need to select a category to display the Search Ads page; from this page, click the Place Ad link.

3. Choose the category in which you wish to place an ad.

4. When the Place Ad page appears, select a specific subcategory.

5. When the sign-in page appears, enter your User ID and Password and click Continue. (If you're a first-time visitor, click the I Need a User ID link and follow the directions there; you'll need to supply some personal information, including your name and email address.)

6. When the next page appears, follow the category-specific instructions for placing your ad.

Your new ad should appear online within 24 hours; you'll be notified via email when anyone answers your ad.

FINDING ROMANCE IN THE PERSONAL ADS

In addition to normal classified ads, Lycos also lets you place and respond to personal ads. Lycos personals are a great way to meet compatible people in your area; just follow these instructions to meet your potential soulmate:

1. Go to the main Lycos Classifieds page by clicking the Classifieds link on the main Lycos Web page, or directly at www.lycos.com/shopnet/classifieds.

2. From the Lycos Classifieds page, click the Personals link.

3. When the Search Ads page appears (see Figure 20.2), select any or all of the following criteria: Area, Looking For (Women Seeking Men, Men Seeking Women, and so on), Relationship, Ethnicity, Religion, Age Range, Smokes, Drinks, Has Children, Wants Children.

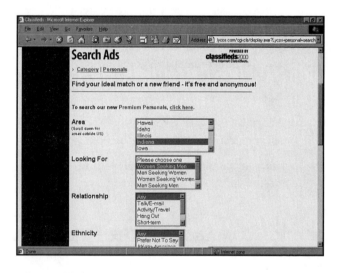

FIGURE 20.2
Use Lycos Personals to select all the qualities you want in a potential mate.

TIP

You don't have to select all criteria to make a match, but the more items you choose the closer your match will be.

4. Select Show Newest Ads First to display the most recent ads, then click Search.

5. Lycos will now display a list of ads in your area that match the qualities you're looking for. Click an individual ad header to display that person's entire ad.

6. To correspond with an individual, click the Send Message button and follow the onscreen instructions to compose and send an email message.

Placing a personal ad is just like placing a classified ad; make sure you remember your User ID and password for future use.

TIP

It's best to play it safe when corresponding with and ultimately meeting people you find through online personal ads. For example, you don't have to give out your real email address; you can select to send your message anonymously from the Send Message page, and Lycos will forward any replies to your email box without letting the respondents know your actual email. If you decide to physically meet someone after corresponding with them, choose a public place during the daytime, and make sure one of your friends knows where you are. *Don't* meet someone at his or her home on the first date—keep it public, keep it casual, and always have an "escape" planned if things don't turn out as you'd like.

ANOTHER WAY TO BUY AND SELL— ONLINE AUCTIONS

An online classified ad is a great way to sell an item at a fixed price—but what if you could get several potential buyers bidding for your merchandise at the highest price? Better yet, what if there were a place where you could search for and bid on collectibles and other types of items? What if there was a kind of online "auction" where you try to get the best deals possible, as either a buyer or a seller?

Well, there *are* online auction sites, and they're among the most popular sites on the entire World Wide Web. Here's how a typical online auction works:

1. You begin (either as a buyer or seller) by establishing a no-charge membership with the auction site.

2. The seller creates an ad for an item and lists the item on the auction site. (The auction site typically charges a small fee for each listing, anywhere from 25 cents to 2 dollars.) In the ad, the seller specifies the length of the auction (anywhere from three days to two weeks), and the minimum bid he or she will accept.

3. Potential buyers, searching for a particular type of item (or just browsing through all the merchandise listed in a specific category) read the ad and decide to make a bid. The bidder specifies the *maximum* amount he or she will pay; this amount has to be above the seller's *minimum* bid.

4. Software at the online auction site automatically places a bid for the bidder that bests the current bid by a specified amount—but doesn't reveal the bidder's maximum bid. For example, the current bid on an item might be $25. A bidder is willing to pay up to $40 for the item, and enters a maximum bid of $40. The "proxy" software places a bid for the new bidder in the amount of $26—higher than the current bid, but less than the specified maximum bid. If there are no other bids, this buyer will win the auction with a $26 bid. Other potential buyers, however, can place additional bids; unless their maximum bids are more than the current bidder's $40 maximum, they will be informed that they have been outbid—and the first bidder's current bid will be automatically raised to match the new bids (up to the specified maximum bid price).

5. At the conclusion of an auction, the high bidder is informed of his or her winning bid. The seller is responsible for contacting the high bidder and arranging payment between them. When the seller receives the buyer's payment (generally by check or money order), the seller then ships the merchandise directly to the buyer.

6. Concurrent with the close of the auction, the auction site bills the seller for a small percentage (generally one or two percent) of the final bid price. This fee is directly billed to the seller's credit card.

The most popular online auction site is eBay (www.ebay.com). eBay, shown in Figure 20.3, has literally hundreds of thousands of listings at any given time, and over a million registered users.

To give you an idea of the kinds of items auctioned at eBay, I just did a search for "Batman" merchandise, and found over 1,700 different items listed, from comic books to action figures to original artwork to Pez dispensers! I've used eBay to buy and sell classic model kits, laserdiscs, animation cells, and other types of collectibles. If you have something to sell—or like hunting for stuff at garage sales and flea markets—eBay is worth checking out!

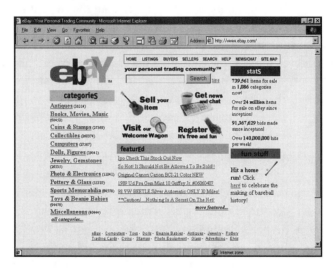

FIGURE 20.3
Search eBay for that collectible item you've been looking for—then hope you bid high enough to win!

ONCE YOU'VE FOUND WHAT YOU WANT IN THE CLASSIFIEDS...

Now that you've learned how to buy and sell items via online classified ads and auctions, it's time for a little personal communication. Turn to Chapter 21, "Using Outlook Express for Email," to learn how to send and receive email using Microsoft's Outlook Express.

PART V

COMMUNICATING WITH EMAIL

CHAPTER 21

USING OUTLOOK EXPRESS
FOR EMAIL

Microsoft's Outlook Express is the email program included with both Internet Explorer 4 and Windows 98. It's a
very versatile email program—so versatile, in fact, that it
also handles USENET newsgroup postings! (See Chapter
25, "Using Outlook Express for Newsgroups.")

Outlook Express and Netscape Messenger are very similar programs, and both perform pretty much the same
functions in the same fashion. There are also other email
programs—both commercial and freeware/shareware—
that you can use for your email correspondence, such as
the popular Eudora program. But if you're a Windows 98
user, you probably want to use the program that came
with your operating system, and Outlook Express is it.

CONFIGURING OUTLOOK EXPRESS FOR
EMAIL

Before you can send and receive email, you first have to
configure Outlook Express for your particular email
account provided by your Internet Service Provider. To

add a new email account to Outlook Express, you'll need to have the following information handy:

➤ Your email address (in the form of *xxx@xxx.xxx*) for the new account

➤ The names of the new account's incoming and outgoing email servers (may be the same)

➤ The new email POP account name and password

TIP

If you used the Internet Connection Wizard to create your Internet connection when you first installed Windows, Outlook Express was automatically configured at that time.

Follow these steps to configure Outlook Express for your ISP:

1. Click the Launch Outlook Express icon on the Quick Launch toolbar to launch Outlook Express.

2. Pull down the Tools menu and select Accounts.

3. When the Internet Accounts dialog box appears, click the Mail tab, and then click the Add button and select Mail.

4. Outlook Express now launches a subset of the Internet Connection Wizard. Follow the on-screen instructions to complete your new account's configuration.

If you have more than one email account with multiple ISPs, repeat these steps to add your additional accounts.

READING AN EMAIL MESSAGE

If you've received new email messages, they will be stored
in Outlook Express' Inbox. To read a new message:

1. Click the Inbox icon in the Outlook Bar (or pull
down the Go menu and select Inbox). All waiting
messages will now appear in the message pane.

2. Click the message header of the message you want to
read to display the contents of the message in the
preview pane (see Figure 21.1).

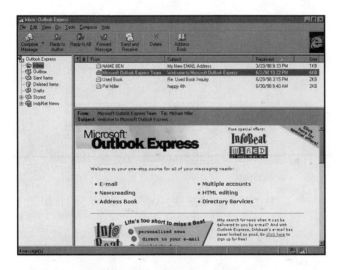

FIGURE 21.1
*To view a message in the Inbox, click the message header in the message pane;
the contents are displayed in the preview pane.*

3. To display the message in a separate window, double-
click the message in the message pane.

TIP

Some email messages have additional files—like Word documents or graphics files—"attached" to the mail message. To open an attached file, right-click the file icon and select Open; to save an attached file to your hard disk, right-click the file icon and select Save As.

REPLYING TO AN EMAIL MESSAGE

Replying to an email message is as easy as clicking a button. Just follow these steps:

1. In the message pane, click the message header to which you wish to reply.

2. Click the Reply to Author button on the toolbar. (Alternately, you can click the Reply to All button to reply to all recipients of the message, not just the message sender—or you can click on the Forward button to send the message to a completely different recipient.)

3. A Re: window appears. The original message sender is now listed in the To box, with the original message's subject referenced in the Subject box. The original message is "quoted" in the text area of the window, with > preceding the original text.

4. Type your reply in the text area above the quoted text.

5. Click the Send button to send this reply to your Outbox.

6. To send the message from your Outbox over the Internet to your recipient's inbox, click the Send and Receive button.

CREATING A NEW EMAIL MESSAGE

Use Outlook Express to create all your mail messages and take advantage of features like spell checking and formatting. To create a new email message, follow these steps:

1. Click the Outlook Express icon on the Outlook Bar.
2. Click the Compose Message button on the toolbar.
3. When the New Message dialog box appears (see Figure 21.2), enter the email address of the recipient(s) in the To: field and the address of anyone you want to receive a carbon copy into the Cc: box. Separate multiple addresses with a semicolon (;) but no spaces, like this:

   `mmiller@mcp.com;gjetson@sprockets.com.`

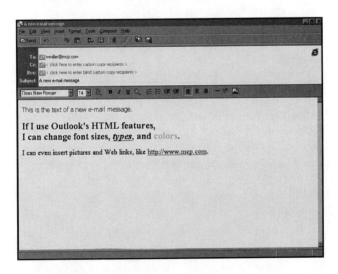

FIGURE 21.2

Creating a new email message; enter the recipient's address in the To: field, the topic of the message in the Subject field, and the text of the message in the big text area.

4. You can also select names from your Address Book by clicking the Address Book button on the toolbar. When the Select Recipients dialog box appears, select the name(s) of whomever you want to send the message to and click the To: button. Select the name(s) of whomever you want to send a carbon copy of the message to and click the Cc: button. Click OK when done.

5. Enter the subject of the message in the Subject field.

6. Move your cursor to the main message area and type your message.

7. You can choose to send your message in either plain text or HTML format. If you choose to send it in HTML format, you can use the formatting buttons on the toolbar to add boldface, italic, underlined, or aligned text. To select HTML formatting, pull down the Format menu and select Rich Text (HTML).

TIP

HTML text formatting in email messages works only when your recipient is using Outlook Express, Microsoft Exchange mail, Netscape Messenger, or another HTML-enabled email program. If your recipient is using a non-HTML email program (such as cc:Mail), all text formatting will be lost.

8. If you're sending the message in HTML format, you can add background colors and graphics. If you simply want to use a background color, pull down the Format menu, select Background, select Color, and then pick a color from the color list. If you want to use a background picture, pull down the Format menu, select Background, and select Picture. When the Background Picture dialog box appears, enter the name of the graphics file you want to use, and then click OK.

9. When your message is complete, send it to the Outbox by clicking the Send button.

10. To send the message from your Outbox over the Internet to your recipient's inbox, click the Send and Receive button.

TIP

If you want to send a file to someone over the Internet, the easiest way to do so is to attach that file to an email message. After you've created a new message, click the Attachment button (looks like a paper clip) on the toolbar. When the Insert Attachment dialog box appears, locate the file you want to send and click Attach. The attached file now appears as an icon in a new pane under the main text pane of your message, and will be sent along with your normal message when you click the Send button.

ONCE YOU'VE MASTERED EMAIL WITH OUTLOOK EXPRESS...

Now that you've learned how to use Outlook Express to send and receive email messages, it's time to learn how to use email to communicate with groups of people with similar interests. Turn to Chapter 24, "Communicating in Email Mailing Lists," to learn how to subscribe to email mailing lists.

CHAPTER 22

USING NETSCAPE MESSENGER FOR EMAIL

Netscape Messenger is the email program included with the Netscape Communicator suite. It's a versatile email program that also handles USENET newsgroup postings (see Chapter 26, "Using Netscape Messenger for Newsgroups").

Netscape Messenger is very similar to Microsoft's Outlook Express; they both perform pretty much the same functions in pretty much the same fashion. There are also other email programs—both commercial and freeware/shareware—that you can also use for your email correspondence, such as the popular Eudora program. But if you're a Netscape user, chances are you're using Messenger for all your email needs.

CONFIGURING NETSCAPE MESSENGER FOR EMAIL

Before you can send and receive email, you first have to configure Netscape Messenger for your particular email account provided by your Internet Service Provider. To

add a new email account to Netscape Messenger, you'll
need to have the following information handy:

➤ Your email address (in the form of *xxx@xxx.xxx*) for
the new account

➤ The names of the new account's incoming and outgoing email servers (may be the same)

➤ The new email POP account name and password

Follow these steps to configure Messenger for your ISP:

1. Click the Windows Start button, select Programs,
select Netscape Communicator, then select Netscape
Messenger to launch Messenger.

2. Pull down the Edit menu and select Preferences.

3. When the Preferences dialog box appears, open the
Mail & Newsgroups section of the Category tree.

4. Select Identity from the Category tree, and enter
your name and email address in the proper boxes.

5. Select Mail Servers from the Category tree and click
the Add button.

6. When the Mail Server Properties dialog box appears,
select the General tab and enter the server name,
type (generally POP3), and your user name. Click
OK when done.

7. Enter the name of your outgoing mail server in the
Outgoing Mail Server box.

8. Click OK when done.

TIP

If you haven't yet configured Messenger, you will be prompted
to complete the Mail & Newsgroups Wizard when you first

open your Inbox; this Wizard takes you through the same steps as described above.

READING AN EMAIL MESSAGE

If you've received new email messages, they will be stored in Messenger's Inbox. To read a new message:

1. Click the Inbox icon in the Folders list. All waiting messages will now appear in the Message pane.

2. Click the message header of the message you want to read to display the contents of the message in the preview pane (see Figure 22.1).

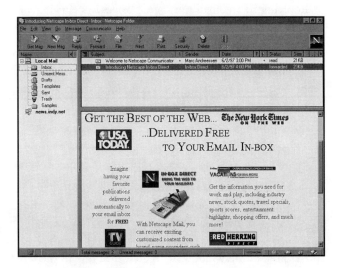

FIGURE 22.1
To view a message in the Inbox, click the message header in the message pane; the contents are displayed in the preview pane.

3. To display the message in a separate window, double-click the message in the Message pane.

TIP

Some email messages have additional files—such as Word documents or graphics files—"attached" to the mail message; this is indicated by the message text including an attachment button. Click the attachment button to display an Attachment pane; the attached file will be displayed in this new pane. To open the attached file, right-click the file icon (in the Attachment pane) and select Open Attachment; to save the attached file to your hard disk, right-click the file icon and select Save Attachment As.

REPLYING TO AN EMAIL MESSAGE

Replying to an email message is as easy as clicking a button. Just follow these steps:

1. In the Message pane, click the message header to which you wish to reply.

2. Click the Reply button on the toolbar. (Alternately, you can click the Reply All button to reply to all recipients of the message, not just the message sender—or you can click on the Forward button to send the message to a completely different recipient.)

3. A Composition window appears. The original message sender is now listed in the To box, with the original message's subject referenced in the Subject box. The original message is "quoted" in the text area of the window, with a vertical line to the left of the original text.

4. Type your reply in the text area above the quoted text.

5. Click the Send button to send this reply across the Internet.

CREATING A NEW EMAIL MESSAGE

Use Netscape Messenger to create all your mail messages; just follow these steps:

1. Click the Local Mail icon on the Folders list.

2. Click the New Msg button on the toolbar.

3. When the Composition dialog box appears (see Figure 22.2), enter the email address of the recipient(s) in the To: field. If you want someone to receive a carbon copy of the message, pull down the To: button and select Cc:, then enter an address into the Cc: field. To enter multiple addresses, press Enter in between addresses.

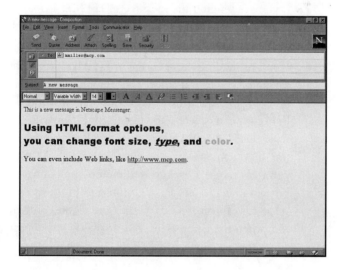

FIGURE 22.2
Creating a new email message: enter the recipient's address in the To: field, the topic of the message in the Subject box, and the text of the message in the big text area.

4. You can also select names from your Address Book by clicking the Address button on the toolbar. When the Select Addresses dialog box appears, select Personal Address Book in the Directory pane, then select the name(s) of whomever you want to send the message to in the right-hand pane. Click the To: button to add this person to your recipient list; click the Cc: button to send this person a carbon copy; click the Bcc: button to send this person a "blind" carbon copy. Click OK when done.

5. Enter the subject of the message in the Subject box.

6. Move your cursor to the main message area and type your message.

7. If you are sending the message in HTML format, you can use the formatting buttons on the toolbar to add boldface, italic, underlined, or aligned text.

8. If you're sending the message in HTML format, you can add background colors and graphics. If you simply want to use a background color, pull down the Format menu, select Page Colors and Properties, select Use Custom Colors, click the Background button, pick a color from the color list, and click OK. If you want to use a background picture, pull down the Format menu, select Page Colors and Properties, select Use Image, and then click the Choose File button; when the Choose Image File dialog box appears, select the graphics file you want to use, and then click OK.

9. When your message is complete, send it across the Internet by clicking the Send button.

TIP

When you click the Send button for a message that contains HTML text formatting, you will see a dialog box that asks if you want to send the message in HTML, Plain Text, or both HTML and Plain Text. Unless you're sure the recipient is using an HTML-compatible email program (such as Netscape Messenger, Outlook Express, or Microsoft Exchange mail), select to send in both HTML and Plain Text.

TIP

If you want to send a file to someone over the Internet, the easiest way to do so is to attach that file to an email message. After you've created a new message, click the Attach button on the toolbar and select File. When the Enter File to Attach dialog box appears, locate the file you want to send and click Open. The attached file will be sent along with your normal message when you click the Send button.

Once You've Mastered Email with Netscape Messenger...

Now that you've learned how to use Netscape Messenger to send and receive email messages, it's time to learn how to use email to communicate with groups of people with similar interests. Turn to Chapter 24, "Communicating in Email Mailing Lists," to learn how to subscribe to email mailing lists.

CHAPTER 23

USING LYCOSMAIL

While most users get a free email account from their Internet Service Provider, there are several reasons why you might want to create a second, Web-based email account.

First, unlike traditional email, Web-based email can be accessed from any computer, using any Web browser. If you travel a lot, it's easy to access your email from wherever you are just by going to a Web page and entering your username and password.

Second, many users like the idea of having a second email account, often under a different (or assumed) name. This way you can send your "official" correspondence to your ISP-based or work-based email account, and "unofficial" correspondence to your second, Web-based email account.

Finally, there's no harm in setting up a Web-based email account with Lycos—since LycosMail is available free of charge!

> **TIP**
>
> LycosMail is just one of many Web-based email services, including the very popular Hotmail service (`www.hotmail.com`).

SIGNING UP FOR A LYCOSMAIL ACCOUNT

Before you can access LycosMail, you have to sign up for a free LycosMail account. Just follow these steps:

1. Go to the LycosMail home page at `www.lycosemail.com`—or by clicking on the **Get Email** link on the Lycos home page.

2. Click the `New users sign up here!` link.

3. On page one, you get to choose your email address. Enter the first part of your chosen address (the part before the "@") in the a. section of the page. Select a domain (the part of the address *after* the "@") from the choices in the b. section of the page. Click the Next button when ready.

4. On page two, you select where you want to receive your LycosMail messages. If you want to use LycosMail as your main email system, click the Store My Email button. If you want to have all LycosMail messages forwarded to another email system, enter the forwarding email address and click the Forward My Email button.

5. On page three, you must enter a variety of personal information. You also get to select your password for the LycosMail system. Click the Activate button when finished.

After your account is activated, you're presented with the option of selecting various types of information that can be automatically sent to your LycosMail in-box via "canned" email messages. You don't have to select any of these, although the InfoBeat service—which mails you news capsules personalized to your own personal preferences—is popular with some users.

ACCESSING YOUR LYCOSMAIL ACCOUNT

Now that you have your LycosMail account activated, it's time to access your new account. Just follow these steps:

1. Go to the LycosMail login page at
`www.lycosemail.com/member/login.page`.

2. Enter your new LycosMail address and password in the corresponding boxes. (Remember to enter your *complete* email address, including the domain after the "@".)

3. Click the Login button.

You're now presented with the LycosMail Welcome page, where you can send and receive email messages.

READING AND REPLYING TO MESSAGES WITH LYCOSMAIL

If you have messages waiting, your LycosMail Welcome page (shown in Figure 23.1) will indicate the number of messages in your Inbox folder. To read and reply to waiting messages, follow these steps:

1. Click the Inbox link to display the contents of your Inbox folder.

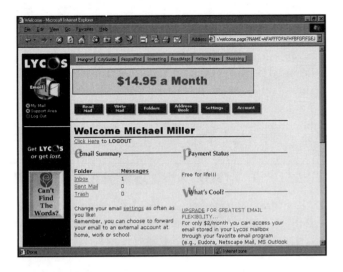

FIGURE 23.1
The LycosMail Welcome page; the number of waiting messages will be displayed in your Inbox folder.

2. Click on the subject of the message you want to read. The full message is now displayed on a new Web page.

3. To reply to this message, click the Reply link. When the New Message page appears, The original message sender is now listed in the To: box, with the original message's subject referenced in the Subject: box. The original message is "quoted" in the text area of the window, with > preceding the original text; type your reply in the text area above the quoted text, then click the Send This Email button.

4. To delete this message, click the Delete link.

5. To store this message in another folder, select a folder from the Move This Message To: list, then click the Move button.

6. To return to your Inbox without deleting or moving the message, click the Close link.

Get into the habit of doing something with your messages (deleting or moving them) as soon as you read them; too many previously read messages can clog up your LycosMail Inbox folder.

CREATING AND SENDING A LYCOSMAIL MESSAGE

To use LycosMail to create a new email message, follow these steps:

1. Click the Write Mail button.

2. When the New Message page appears (see Figure 23.2), enter the recipient's address in the To: box, enter the subject of the message in the Subject: box, enter the address of any carbon copy recipients in the Cc: box, and enter the address of any blind carbon copy recipients in the Bcc: box.

3. Enter the text of your message in the Mail Body box.

4. To attach a file to the message, click the Browse button at the bottom of the page; when the Choose File dialog appears, select the file to attach, then click Open. (You can send up to 500K worth of files with each message.)

5. When the message is complete, click the Send This Email button at the bottom of the page.

As you can see, LycosMail works pretty much like Outlook Express or Netscape Messenger, except that it works from within your Web browser over the World Wide Web. It's really an easy way to manage your messages!

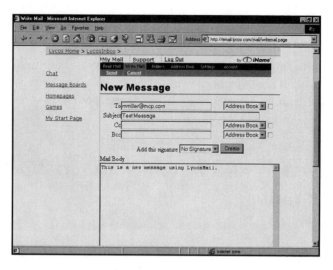

FIGURE 23.2
Compose your LycosMail message on the New Message page.

ONCE YOU'VE MASTERED LYCOSMAIL...

Now that you've learned how to use LycosMail to send and receive email messages, it's time to learn how to use email to communicate with groups of people with similar interests. Turn to Chapter 24, "Communicating in Email Mailing Lists," to learn how to subscribe to email mailing lists.

CHAPTER 24

COMMUNICATING IN EMAIL MAILING LISTS

Another neat thing about email on the Internet is the existence of special-interest *mailing lists*. There are literally thousands of these lists, which are run by *list managers* who encourage discussion and debate on selected topics by a variety of different users. For example, if you're interested in Marilyn Monroe, you can subscribe to the Marilyn Monroe mailing list. From time to time you'll receive (via email) a batch of messages from other mailing list members interested in Marilyn Monroe; you can also send mail to other members of the group.

Mailing lists are similar to USENET newsgroups in that they both serve as gathering places for people with similar interests. The main difference is that mailing lists tend to be a little more organized and focus on more specific topics, while newsgroups are open forums in which anyone can participate. Most mailing lists have fewer members than many newsgroups because a single individual must moderate mailing lists. Newsgroups, as you'll find out in Part VI, "Communicating in Newsgroups," don't have much moderation at all!

Retrieving a List of Mailing Lists

Before you can subscribe to an email mailing list you
need to know a little bit about the list—and you need to
know which lists are available! Fortunately, there are Web
sites that maintain "lists of lists." Follow these steps to
access one of the most popular mailing list sites:

1. Use your Web browser to go to the Web page for
   Liszt, the Mailing List Directory, located at the following address: www.liszt.com (see Figure 24.1).

Figure 24.1
*Use Liszt (www.liszt.com) to find the mailing lists to which you want to sub-
scribe.*

2. Navigate to the subject you're interested in by clicking on the appropriate links. (You can also use the
   search form to search through Liszt's list of over
   80,000 lists.)

3. All mailing lists for your desired topic are now displayed. Details for each list include instructions on how to subscribe.

New mailing lists are created every day; return to this page often for new listings.

TIP

There are several other Web sites that contain lists of email mailing lists, including The List of Lists (www.catalog.com/vivian/interest-group-search.html) and Publicly Accessible Mailing Lists (www.neosoft.com/internet/paml/bysubj.html).

SUBSCRIBING TO A MAILING LIST

To subscribe to an email mailing list, you must send email to the list manager noting that you want to become a member. You have to follow a particular format in your message, however. Just follow these steps:

1. Using your email program, create a new email message.

2. In the To: field, enter the email address of the mailing list.

3. In the Subject: field, enter **SUBSCRIBE**.

TIP

The following instructions work for most mailing lists, but not all. Be sure to read and follow the specific instructions for each particular mailing list to which you want to subscribe.

---

4. For the text of the message, enter **SUBSCRIBE** *list-name firstname lastname* as the text of your message, where *listname* is the name of the mailing list, and *firstname* and *lastname* are your first and last names.

5. When you are finished typing, click the Send button to send the message and register your subscription. Once you subscribe to a mailing list, you should begin receiving mail from this list within two or three days.

T I P

Sometimes a mailing list has one address for subscribing and a different address for normal posting. Try not to get these confused!

If you want to cancel a mailing list subscription, send a similar message to the list with **UNSUBSCRIBE** as the subject and **UNSUBSCRIBE** *listname* as the message text.

ONCE YOU'VE MASTERED EMAIL MAILING LISTS...

Now that you've learned how to find and subscribe to email mailing lists, it's time to open up a whole new world of Internet communities. Turn to either Chapter 25 or Chapter 26 to learn all about USENET newsgroups.

PART VI

PART VI

COMMUNICATING IN NEWSGROUPS

CHAPTER 25

USING OUTLOOK EXPRESS FOR NEWSGROUPS

In addition to being .an email program, Outlook Express also functions as a newsreader for USENET newsgroups. A newsgroup is an electronic gathering place for people with similar interests. Within a newsgroup users post messages (called *articles*) about a variety of topics; other users read these articles and, when so disposed, respond. The result is a kind of on-going, freeform discussion, in which dozens—or hundreds—of users may participate.

TIP

There are several major *hierarchies* of newsgroups; it pays to know what kinds of newsgroups you'll find in which hierarchies. The major hierarchies are as follows:

> **alt**—alternative topics

> **bit**—LISTSERV mailing lists from the BITNET network

> **biz**—business-oriented product announcements

> **comp**—computer-related topics

continues

> ➤ **k12**—topics related to kindergarten through 12th grade education
>
> ➤ **misc**—miscellaneous topics
>
> ➤ **rec**—recreational topics of all sorts, from sports to books
>
> ➤ **sci**—science topics
>
> ➤ **soc**—topics related to social issues
>
> ➤ **talk**—conversational (and controversial) topics

CONFIGURING OUTLOOK EXPRESS FOR NEWSGROUPS

Before you can use Outlook Express to read and send newsgroup messages, you first must configure it for your specific Internet connection. If you used the Internet Connection Wizard to create your Internet connection, Outlook Express was automatically configured at that time; if you didn't use the Internet Connection Wizard to configure Outlook Express, you'll need to configure Outlook Express manually for your newsgroup server.

TIP

Before you add a new newsgroup account to Outlook Express, you'll need to know the name of the account's news server, which your ISP will provide.

1. From within Outlook Express, pull down the <u>T</u>ools menu and select <u>A</u>ccounts.

2. When the Internet Accounts dialog box appears, click the News tab, click the Add button, and then select News.

3. Outlook Express now launches a subset of the Internet Connection Wizard. Follow the on-screen instructions to complete your account configuration.

SELECTING AND SUBSCRIBING TO NEWSGROUPS

After you're connected to your news server, you can choose from over 25,000 newsgroups to monitor. You can simply go to selected newsgroups, or you can "subscribe" to selected newsgroups. When you subscribe to a newsgroup, there is no formal registration process; this simply means you've added this newsgroup to a list of your favorites that you can access without searching all 25,000 groups.

1. From within Outlook Express, click the icon in the Folder List for your particular news server. (If you already have the newsreader section of Outlook Express open, just click the Newsgroups button on the toolbar.)

2. If you are not currently subscribed to any newsgroups, you'll be prompted to view a list of all newsgroups. Click Yes and proceed to step 4.

3. If you have already subscribed to one or more newsgroups, you'll now see a list of your subscribed newsgroups. Double-click on a newsgroup to view its contents, or click the Newsgroups button on the toolbar to view a list of all available newsgroups.

4. When the Newsgroups dialog box appears (see Figure 25.1), click the All tab (at the bottom of the dialog box) and select a newsgroup from the main list. You can scroll through the list or search for a specific group by entering key words in the Display Newsgroups Which Contain box.

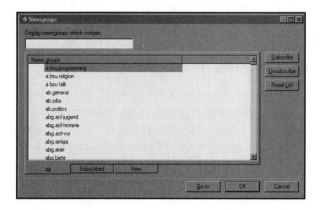

FIGURE 25.1
Search through more than 25,000 different newsgroups for the topic you're interested in.

5. If you want to add this newsgroup to your subscribed list, click the Subscribe button (or double-click the newsgroup item).

6. To choose a newsgroup from your subscribed list, click the Subscribed tab and select the newsgroup you want to read.

7. To go directly to the selected newsgroup, click the Go To button; all the articles from that group appear in the Message pane.

8. Click on a message header to read the contents of the message in the Preview pane.

Once you've entered a newsgroup, you can then view articles, respond to articles, and create and post your own articles.

CREATING AND POSTING NEW NEWSGROUP ARTICLES

Use Outlook Express to create new newsgroup articles, which you can then post to one or more newsgroups. Just follow these steps:

1. From within Outlook Express, click the icon in the Folder List for your particular news server.

2. Select the newsgroup to which you wish to post.

3. Click the Compose Message button. When the New Message window appears, the selected newsgroup is displayed in the Newsgroups field.

4. To post to other newsgroups, click the icon in the newsgroups field. When the Pick Newsgroups dialog box appears, select one or more newsgroups from the list, click the Add button, then click OK. (To display all newsgroups, deselect Show Only Subscribed Newsgroups.)

5. Enter a subject in the Subject field, then type the text of your article in the main window.

6. Click the Post button to post this article to the selected newsgroup(s).

Newsgroup users have a strict code of ethics that you don't want to violate. If you are unfamiliar with newsgroups, you may want to just read for a while before you start posting your own messages. When you do decide to participate, remember that advertising can be done only in the context of the topic (if in doubt, don't do it), typing in UPPERCASE is frowned upon, and you shouldn't "spam" multiple newsgroups with identical messages. If you engage in any of these behaviors, you run the risk of being "flamed" by irate users sending you gobs and gobs of hate mail.

VIEWING AND SAVING ATTACHED FILES

Many newsgroups exist to distribute files—generally graphics or sound files. These files are stored in *binary* format (so-called because if you looked at the raw, coded file, it would look like a series of binary numbers). Most of the newsgroups specializing in these files are in the **alt.binaries** hierarchy.

> **TIP**
>
> Many of the **alt.binaries** newsgroups contain adult images—particularly those in the **alt.binaries.pictures.erotica** hierarchy. You should monitor your children to make sure they don't access these groups by mistake—or on purpose!

Outlook Express lets you view graphics files right in the preview pane; you can also save attached files to your hard disk. If an article contains an attachment, you'll see a "paper clip" icon in the article header. To view and save attached files to your hard disk, follow these steps:

1. To view a graphics attachment, click the article header that includes the attachment. The graphic should display in the preview pane, as shown in Figure 25.2.

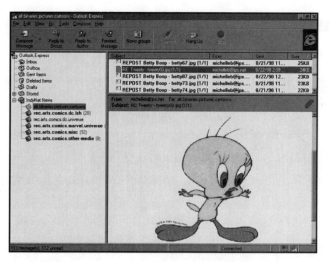

FIGURE 25.2
A newsgroup article containing a graphic image; browse through the alt.bina-ries.pictures hierarchy for a list of newsgroups specializing in pictures and graphics.

2. To save an attachment to your hard disk, click the article header that includes the attachment. Pull down the File menu and select Save Attachments, and then select the file you want to save. When the Save Attachment As dialog box appears, select a location for the file and click Save.

You can also choose to view attached files through their associated programs. Just click the paperclip icon in the preview pane header and select the file you wish to view; the associated application will automatically launch and display the selected file.

ATTACHING FILES TO NEWSGROUP ARTICLES

Outlook Express lets you attach files to newsgroup articles you post. This is particularly useful if you frequent any of the "binaries" picture-oriented newsgroups. Just follow these steps:

1. Create a new newsgroup article.
2. Click the Attachment button (looks like a paper clip) on the toolbar.
3. When the Insert Attachment dialog box appears, locate the file you want to send and click Attach. The attached file appears as an icon in a new pane under the main text pane of your message.
4. Click the Post button to post the article with the attachment to the select newsgroup(s).

When you post articles containing attachments, try to keep the file size as small as possible—large file attachments consume lots of bandwidth and disk space on the Internet itself, on host servers, and on the PCs of people downloading your article.

ONCE YOU'VE MASTERED USENET NEWSGROUPS...

Now that you've learned how to use Outlook Express to read and post articles to newsgroups, it's time to find out how to search for specific information across multiple newsgroups. Turn to Chapter 27, "Searching Lycos for Newsgroups," to learn how to use Lycos to search newsgroup archives.

CHAPTER 26

USING NETSCAPE MESSENGER FOR NEWSGROUPS

Netscape Messenger, like Outlook Express, functions as both an email program and a newsreader for USENET newsgroups. As with Outlook Express, you need to configure Netscape Messenger for newsgroup use, and learn how to read and post newsgroup articles. In many ways, Messenger functions in a similar fashion to Outlook Express when accessing USENET newsgroups.

TIP

In addition to Netscape Messenger and Outlook Express, there are several other popular newsreader programs available, most of them available as either shareware or freeware programs. Some of the most popular include **Free Agent**, **NewsMonger**, **NewsXPress**, and **WinVN**. All of these programs can be found in the Tucows software library on the mcp.com Web site (tucows.mcp.com).

CONFIGURING NETSCAPE MESSENGER FOR NEWSGROUPS

Before you can use Netscape Messenger to read and send newsgroup messages, you first must configure it for your specific Internet connection. Just follow these steps:

TIP

Before you add a new newsgroup account to Netscape Messenger, you'll need to know the name of the account's news server, which will be provided by your ISP.

1. From within Netscape Messenger, pull down the Edit menu and select Preferences.

2. When the Preferences dialog box appears, open the Mail & Newsgroups section of the Category tree.

3. Select Newsgroup Servers from the Category tree and click the Add button.

4. When the Newsgroup Server Properties dialog box appears,enter the name of your newsgroup server in the Server box.

5. Click OK when done.

SELECTING AND SUBSCRIBING TO NEWSGROUPS

After you're connected to your news server, you can choose from over 25,000 newsgroups to monitor. You can simply go to selected newsgroups, or you can "subscribe" to selected newsgroups. When you subscribe to a newsgroup, there is no formal registration process; this simply means you've added this newsgroup to a list of your favorites that you can access without searching all 25,000 groups.

1. From within Netscape Messenger, click the icon in the Folder List for your particular news server.

2. To view a complete list of all USENET newsgroups, pull down the File menu and select Subscribe.

3. When the Subscribe to Newsgroups dialog box appears (see Figure 26.1), click the All tab to view all newsgroups, or the Search for a Group tab to search for a specific newsgroup.

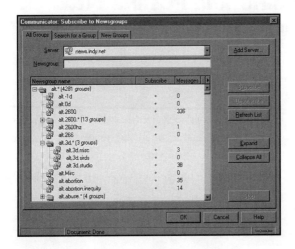

FIGURE 26.1
Search through more than 25,000 different newsgroups for the topic you're interested in.

4. To subscribe to a newsgroup (or groups), select one or more newsgroups and click the Subscribe button. Click OK when done subscribing.

5. When you have subscribed to a newsgroup, it appears under the news server icon in the Folders pane. When you click on a specific newsgroup, all the articles from that group appear in Messenger's Message pane.

6. Click on a message header to read the contents of the message in the preview pane.

Once you've entered a newsgroup, you can then view articles, respond to articles, and create and post your own articles.

CREATING AND POSTING NEW NEWSGROUP ARTICLES

Use Netscape Messenger to create new newsgroup articles, which you can then post to one or more newsgroups. Just follow these steps:

1. From within Netscape Messenger, click the icon in the Folder List to open the newsgroup pane for a particular news server.

2. Click on the newsgroup to which you wish to post.

3. Click the New Msg button. When the Composition window appears, the selected newsgroup is displayed in the Group: field.

4. To post to other newsgroups, enter the names of other newsgroups in the Group: field.

5. Enter a subject in the Subject field, then type the text of your article in the main window.

6. Click the Send button to post this article to the selected newsgroup(s).

Newsgroup users have a strict code of ethics that you don't want to violate. If you are unfamiliar with newsgroups, you may want to just read for a while before you start posting your own messages. When you do decide to participate, remember that advertising can be done only in the context of the topic (if in doubt, don't do it), typing in UPPERCASE is frowned upon, and you shouldn't "spam" multiple newsgroups with identical messages. If you engage in any of these behaviors, you run the risk of being "flamed" by irate users sending you gobs and gobs of hate mail.

VIEWING AND SAVING ATTACHED FILES

Many newsgroups exist to distribute files—generally graphics or sound files. These files are stored in *binary* format (so-called because if you looked at the raw, coded file, it would look like a series of binary numbers). Most of the newsgroups specializing in these files are in the **alt.binaries** hierarchy.

> **TIP**
>
> Many of the **alt.binaries** newsgroups contain adult images—particularly those in the **alt.binaries.pictures.erotica** hierarchy. You should monitor your children to make sure they don't access these groups by mistake—or on purpose!

Netscape Messenger lets you view graphics files right in the preview pane; you can also save attached files to your hard disk. To view and save attached files to your hard disk, just follow these steps:

1. To view a graphics attachment, click the article header that includes the attachment. The graphic should display in the preview pane, as shown in Figure 26.2.

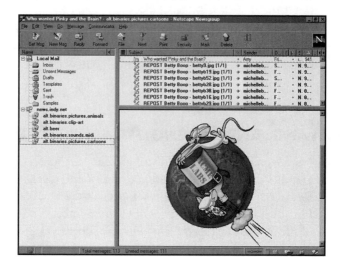

FIGURE 26.2
A newsgroup article containing a graphic image; browse through the alt.binaries.pictures hierarchy for a list of newsgroups specializing in pictures and graphics.

2. To save a graphics attachment to your hard disk, right-click the picture in the preview pane and select Save Image As from the pop-up menu. When the Save As dialog box appears, select a location for the file and click Save.

> **TIP**
>
> If the attachment isn't a graphics file, the filename will be listed as a link in the message's preview pane. To save a non-graphics file, right-click the file link, select Save Link As, and when the Save As dialog box appears, select a location for the file and click Save.

ATTACHING FILES TO NEWSGROUP ARTICLES

Netscape Messenger lets you attach files to newsgroup articles you post. This is particularly useful if you frequent any of the "binaries" picture-oriented newsgroups. Just follow these steps:

1. Create a new newsgroup article.

2. Click the Attach button on the toolbar and select File.

3. When the Enter File to Attach dialog box appears, locate the file you want to send and click Open. The attached file will be sent along with your normal message when you click the Send button.

When you post articles containing attachments, try to keep the file size as small as possible—large file attachments consume lots of bandwidth and disk space on the Internet itself, on host servers, and on the PCs of people downloading your article.

Once You've Mastered USENET Newsgroups...

Now that you've learned how to use Netscape Messenger to read and post articles to newsgroups, it's time to find out how to search for specific information across multiple newsgroups. Turn to Chapter 27, "Searching Lycos for Newsgroups," to learn how to use Lycos to search newsgroup archives.

CHAPTER 27

SEARCHING LYCOS FOR NEWSGROUPS

Subscribing to newsgroups and browsing through individual newsgroup articles is fine if you're trying to participate in an individual newsgroup community. However, if you're just searching for information—and you either don't know or don't care which newsgroups contain that information—then you need a more powerful tool than either Outlook Express or Netscape Messenger.

Lycos is that tool.

Lycos, in addition to letting you search the Web for information, also lets you search USENET newsgroups. You use the same search box as you do normally, but you tell Lycos you want to search USENET newsgroups. Lycos then searches all the newsgroups on USENET for what you want, and returns the results in a form that you'll find very familiar.

TIP

Lycos uses Deja News, a Web site devoted to the archiving of newsgroup articles, to search the USENET archives. If you want additional newsgroup searching power, you may want to go directly to the Deja News Web site (www.dejanews.com), or to SuperNews (www.supernews.com), a similar USENET archive site.

PERFORMING A BASIC NEWSGROUP SEARCH

To use Lycos to search USENET newsgroups, just follow these steps:

1. From the main Lycos Web page (www.lycos.com), click the Search Options link.

2. When the Lycos Pro Search page appears, enter the word or phrase you wish to search for in the Search For: box.

3. In the Look For... section, select Newsgroups.

4. Click the Go Get It button (or press Enter).

Lycos will now automatically retrieve a list of newsgroup articles (from a variety of newsgroups) that match your search criteria. As you can see in Figure 27.1, the results include the article header, newsgroup it was posted in, and the name of the user who posted the article. Click on the article header to read the text of the article.

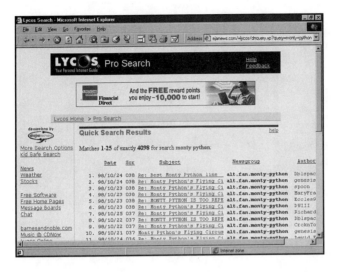

FIGURE 27.1
The results of a Lycos newsgroup search.

READING NEWSGROUP ARTICLES

When you click on an article header on the results page, you display the entire text of the article—plus links to other, related information (see Figure 27.2). This additional information includes:

➤ Previous Article lets you view the previous article in the thread.

TIP

A *thread* is a collection of newsgroup articles on the same subject. Each subsequent post to a thread is in response to a previous article.

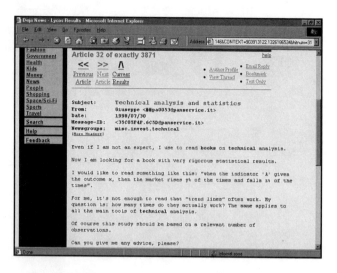

FIGURE 27.2

Reading a newsgroup article—and linking to additional articles and information.

➤ Next Article lets you view the next article in the thread.

➤ Current Results returns you to the previous page of search results.

➤ Author Profile lets you view a complete list of articles (across all newsgroups) posted by the author of the current article.

➤ View Thread lets you view the headers for all the articles in the current thread.

➤ Email Reply lets you send a reply to the poster of this article via email—without posting the reply to the entire newsgroup.

TIP

If the article is past a certain age, you may receive a message that tells you that you can't reply to it.

> ➤ Bookmark simplifies the message's URL so that it can be more easily saved as a Bookmark or Favorite in your Web browser. Click this link *before* you Bookmark the page or save it as a Favorite.

> ➤ Text Only displays the current article in a plain text format without any HTML format. (Use this option if you want to copy the text of the message into another application.)

ONCE YOU'VE MASTERED USENET NEWSGROUPS...

Now that you've learned how to search the USENET archives, you might want to explore another type of online forum. Turn to Chapter 28, "Using Lycos Message Boards," to learn how to use Lycos's message boards.

CHAPTER 28

USING LYCOS MESSAGE BOARDS

USENET newsgroups aren't the only electronic message forums on the Internet. Lycos has its own internal forums for topic-oriented messages, which it calls *Message Boards*.

Lycos Message Boards (found at boards.lycos.com) are part of a sophisticated electronic *bulletin board system* (or BBS, for short). Lycos's BBS includes dozens of different Message Boards, covering topics from Autos to Travel, each of which includes hundreds of articles posted by Lycos users.

ACCESSING LYCOS MESSAGE BOARDS

When you first access Lycos Message Boards, you have the option of continuing into the individual boards as a "guest," or of signing in as a registered user. While you can ready and reply to messages as a guest, you need to register to post new articles or start new threads. To become a registered user, just click the Sign In link on the main Message Boards page (boards.lycos.com) and fill out the form on the following page.

Once you've signed in (or decided to proceed as a guest), follow these steps to access a specific Message Board:

1. Access Lycos Message Boards by clicking the Message Boards link on the main Lycos Web page—or go to boards.lycos.com.

2. When the Message Boards page appears (see Figure 28.1), click on the link to access a specific Message Board. Many message boards have "sub-boards;" click on one of these links to go directly to a more specific board.

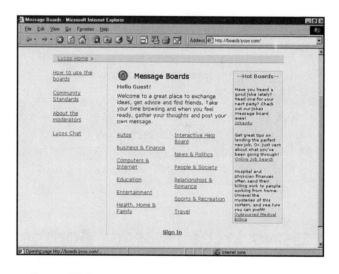

FIGURE 28.1
The master list of Lycos Message Boards.

READING AND REPLYING TO ARTICLES

To read and reply to articles on a specific Message Board,
follow these steps:

1. Within a specific Message Board, messages in a
   thread are displayed one after another on the same
   page, as shown in Figure 28.2.

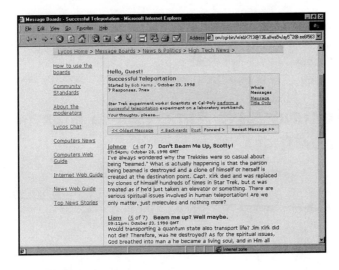

FIGURE 28.2
Reading a Message Board article; click Reply *to post a follow-up article.*

2. To read messages in this thread previous to those displayed on this page, click the Backwards link. To read
   newer messages not yet displayed on this page, click
   the Forward link.

3. To reply to the current article, click the Post link, or just scroll down to the bottom of the current page. Enter the heading for your message in the Title box, add your message to the text box, and click Post My Message to post the reply to the current thread.

T I P

To search for specific articles, enter your search criteria in the Search For: box at the top of any Message Board page, then click Go Get It. Lycos will return a list of articles (from all Message Boards) that match your search criteria.

POSTING NEW ARTICLES AND STARTING NEW THREADS

In addition to replying to existing articles, you can post your own new articles to any Message Board. When you post your article, it becomes the first article in a new thread.

T I P

While you can read and respond to messages without formally registering with Lycos, you need to register before you can start a new message thread.

Just follow these steps:

1. From within a specific Message Board, click the Add Discussion link.

2. When the next page appears (see Figure 28.3), enter the subject of the article in the New Discussion Topic box.

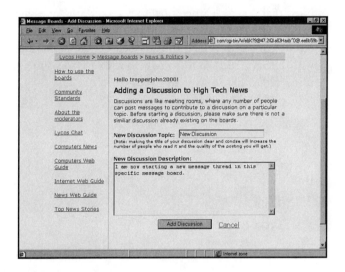

FIGURE 28.3
Posting a new Message Board article.

3. Enter the body of your message into the New Discussion Description text box.

4. When your message is completed, click Add Discussion to post the article to the current Message Board.

ONCE YOU'VE MASTERED LYCOS MESSAGE BOARDS...

Now that you've learned how to read and post messages on Lycos' Message Boards, it's time for some real-time online communication. Turn to Chapter 29, "Chatting with Lycos Chat," to learn how to use carry on conversations with other users with Lycos Chat.

PART VII

COMMUNICATING WITH CHAT

CHAPTER 29

CHATTING WITH LYCOS CHAT

Online Chat is kind of like one of those 900-number telephone chat lines—except you use your keyboard instead
of a telephone, and you don't run up bills at $1.99/minute
or more. When you enter a *Chat room*, you can just "listen" to conversations (called *lurking*), or you can join in
yourself. And you don't have to use your real name (you
use a *nickname* instead), so you can remain as anonymous
as you want.

There are dozens of different sites on the Internet
that operate Chat services. One of the most popular
Chat services on the Web is Lycos Chat, found at
`chat.lycos.com`.

Once you're logged into Lycos Chat, you enter a Chat
room to begin your Chat session. Lycos Chat offers
dozens of different rooms, kind of like the channels on
CB radios. Each Chat room is assigned a specific topic, so
find a room specializing in a topic you're interested in,
then start chatting!

ACCESSING A CHAT ROOM

Lycos Chat has dozens of Chat rooms to choose from, each assigned a specific topic area. Follow these steps to access a specific Chat room and display the Chat window:

> **T I P**
>
> Before you're allowed into a Lycos Chat Room, you'll need to create a new account, which is where you create your initial user profile. Your user profile includes a variety of personal information, including your name, address, and a unique username. You can, at any time, edit your user profile by clicking the Users tab in any Chat window, selecting your own user name, and then clicking the User Profile button.

1. Access Lycos Chat by clicking the People link on the main Lycos Web page (www.lycos.com), then clicking the Chat With New Friends link—or go directly to chat.lycos.com.

2. When the Lycos Chat page appears (see Figure 29.1), select the type of chat you wish to engage in. Typical choices include Romance, Random Chat, Life and Coping, Entertainment, and Current Events.

3. When the next page appears, select the type of Chat *client* you wish to use and click the Enter Now! button.

Lycos now opens up a new Chat window on your desktop, which is where the actual chatting takes place.

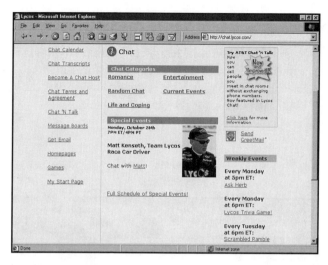

FIGURE 29.1

The main Lycos Chat page; here is where you select the type of Chat you want.

TIP

Lycos lets you use at least three different types of Chat clients, depending on the type of computer system you're using. The **Java Light** client is recommended for most users running an average system: a Pentium® 100MHz or better, connection speeds of 28.8Kbs or better, and a Java-capable browser (such as newer versions of Netscape Navigator or Internet Explorer). The original **Java** client is recommended for users with higher-performance systems: a Pentium® 133MHz or better, connection speeds of 33.6Kbs or better, and a Java-capable browser. The **HTML** client is recommended for users with lower-performance PC systems (as well as anyone connecting from a Macintosh system). Try the Java client first, then the Java Light client; if you can't get either of these Java clients to work, then use the HTML client.

Engaging in a Chat Session

Each of the different Chat clients work pretty much the same way, although the Chat windows presented by each look slightly different. For example, Figure 29.2 shows the Chat window for the Java Chat client.

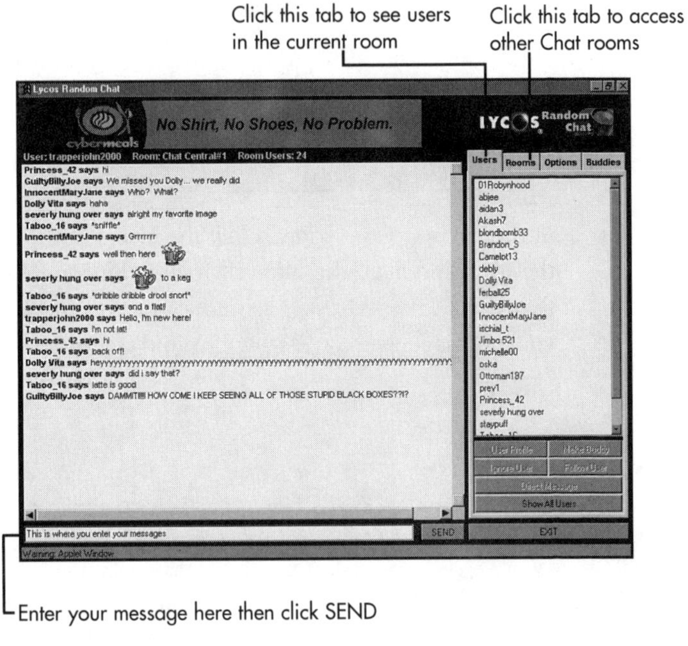
Click this tab to see users in the current room
Click this tab to access other Chat rooms
Lycos Random Chat
No Shirt, No Shoes, No Problem.
User: trapperjohn2000 Room: Chat Central#1 Room Users: 24
Users
Rooms
Options
Buddies
This is where you enter your messages
SEND
EXIT
Enter your message here then click SEND

FIGURE 29.2
Lycos Chat's Java Chat window.

Once the Chat window is open, you can launch right into your Chat session. Just follow these steps:

1. When the Chat window appears, click the Rooms tab, select a Chat room, and click Go To Room.

2. View all messages in the continually scrolling message pane.

3. To add your own message to the Chat session, enter text in the Send box then click the SEND button. Your message will then appear in the message pane.

4. To view information about a particular user, click the Users tab, select the user, and click the User Profile button.

5. To send a private message directly to a specific user in the current Chat room, click the Users tab, select the user, and click the Direct Message button. When the Send Direct Message window appears, enter your message in the Message box and click the SEND button.

When you're done chatting, click the EXIT button to log off from Lycos Chat.

PARTICIPATING IN CHAT EVENTS

In addition to the normal Chat rooms, Lycos Chat also holds larger Chat events, where hundreds of users can chat in real-time on a special topic or to a specific celebrity. These Chat events are held in a special Chat room called the Chat Auditorium. Here's how you access a Chat special event:

1. From the main Lycos Chat page (chat.lycos.com), select the event you wish to participate in, or—if an event is already in progress—go directly to events.lycoschat.com.

2. You are now presented with the Lycos Auditorium page. Enter your username and password (if prompted), then select the type of Chat *client* you wish to use and click the Enter Now! button.

3. If there is a Chat event in session, you will now be presented with a live Chat window for the Auditorium. (If there is no event in session, you'll still see the Chat window, but the Auditorium will be empty.)

4. Proceed to chat as normal, although your messages will be forwarded to a *moderator* who will manage them for presentation to the event's special guest.

SOME TIPS FOR ONLINE CHATTING

Here are some tips to get you started chatting as painlessly as possible:

➤ Don't give out your real name, address, or phone number in any Chat session—period.

➤ Don't assume you're really talking to the person you *think* you're talking to. It's pretty easy to hide behind a nickname and create a totally different persona online.

➤ If you want to get personal with someone you meet in a Chat room, use the Direct Message feature of

Lycos Chat. Don't subject everyone in a room to your private conversations.

➤ Watch out for your kids. The online world is part of the real world, and Chat rooms are good places for unsavory sorts to stalk unknowing youngsters. Make sure that your kids are well informed, that they use good judgment, and that they never, *ever* arrange to meet a chatmate without your supervision.

➤ Spelling and grammar really don't count for much in Chat sessions, but try to at least make your messages understandable. It's also okay to abbreviate in Chat sessions; acronyms work just fine here, IMHO. (IMHO is short for "in my humble opinion," BTW.)

Speaking of acronyms, Table 29.1 gives you a short list of some of the most popular abbreviations you'll find used in online Chat sessions:

Table 29.1 Popular acronyms used in Chat sessions

Acronym	Meaning
AKA	Also known as
ASAP	As soon as possible
BTW	By the way
FWIW	For what it's worth
FYI	For your information
GD&R	Grinning, ducking, and running
IMHO	In my humble opinion
IOW	In other words
LOL	Laughing out loud

continues

Table 29.1 continued

Acronym	Meaning
OTOH	On the other hand
PMJI	Pardon me for jumping in
ROFL	Rolling on the floor laughing
TLA	Three letter acronym
TTFN	Ta ta for now

ONCE YOU'VE MASTERED LYCOS CHAT...

Now that you've learned how to make a pest of yourself in front of dozens of people in a public chat room, it's time to learn how to carry on a private one-on-one online conversation. Turn to Chapter 30, "Instant Messaging with ICQ," to learn how to use the ICQ software for instant messages.

CHAPTER 30

INSTANT MESSAGING WITH ICQ

Chatting, as you learned in the last chapter, is nice, but it's also very public, and very unstructured. What if you just want to "talk" to another online user, in a more private fashion, one-on-one?

Fortunately, there is another method of online communication that is faster than email and more private than chat rooms. *Instant messaging* lets you send short electronic messages back and forth to other online users, in real time, without the need to enter a public chat room.

The most popular instant messaging program, with more than 16 million users, is called *ICQ* (say it out loud—it stands for "I seek you"). ICQ lets you send messages to other ICQ users, engage in private chat sessions with other ICQ users, and even send and receive files to and from other ICQ users, all in real time. (This means that the other user must also be online when you're online; for "offline" communication, use regular email.) ICQ will even let you keep lists of your favorite users, and notify you when they're online.

TIP

ICQ is just one of several "instant messaging" programs.
Another popular program is AOL Instant Messenger, included
in the Netscape Communicator suite.

FINDING, INSTALLING, AND LAUNCHING ICQ

Because ICQ doesn't come pre-installed with either
Netscape Communicator or Internet Explorer, you need
to download a copy of the software from the Internet,
and install it on your machine. It's easy to do this; just
follow these instructions:

1. Use your Web browser to go to the ICQ home page
   at www.icq.com.

2. Click the Download ICQ link, and follow the instructions to download the version for your specific operating system.

TIP

There is one version of ICQ that works for Windows 95,
Windows 98, and Windows NT; this will be the version most
users should download.

3. Once the file is downloaded to your hard disk, click
   the Windows Start button, select Run, and when the
   Run dialog box appears, click the Browse button to

find the downloaded file. (The file should be named **icq*.exe**, where the * will be replaced by letters and numbers specific to your version.) Click OK to run the installation program, and follow the on-screen instructions to complete the installation.

Once ICQ is installed on your computer, there are three ways to launch the program:

➤ Click on the ICQ icon in the Windows Taskbar tray. This will launch ICQ and automatically connect you to the Internet.

➤ Click on the Windows Start button, select Programs, select Mirabilis ICQ, then select ICQ. This will also launch ICQ and automatically connect you to the Internet.

➤ Connect to the Internet through any other method, and ICQ will automatically launch itself. (It detects when you're online, and launches accordingly.)

FINDING OTHER ICQ USERS

Once you're online and ICQ is launched, you see the basic ICQ window, as shown in Figure 30.1. You're now in kind of a "waiting" mode, waiting either for another ICQ user to find you and contact you, or for you to find and contact another ICQ user.

Once you've found another user, ICQ lets you add them to a *Contact List* of your favorite online buddies. Once a name has been added to the Contact List, you can instantly message that person by double-clicking their name; you'll also be notified whenever that user is online.

FIGURE 30.1

The basic ICQ window; click the Add/Find Users button to find other users, or double-click a user's name in the Contact List to send a message.

To find another ICQ user, follow these steps:

1. Click the Add/Find Users button.

2. When the Add/Find Users dialog box appears (see Figure 30.2), click the Main Search button.

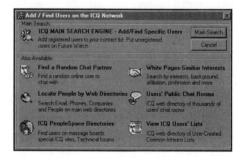

FIGURE 30.2

Seven ways to find other ICQ users; click the Main Search button to search for users with the Contact List Wizard.

3. When the ICQ Global Directory—Contact List Wizard—appears, select to either search by email address, search by nickname or first name, or search by ICQ number. Enter the appropriate search criteria, and click the Next button.

4. The Wizard now returns a list of ICQ users who match your search. Highlight the user you wish to contact.

5. To send a message to this user now, click the Send Message button. When the Send Message dialog box appears, enter your message, then click the Send button.

6. To add this user to your Contact List, click the Next button. When the Add User To Contact List button appears, click OK.

7. When you're returned to the wizard, select Yes to add another user, or No to finish. Click the Next button when done.

In addition to the Contact List Wizard, there are six other ways to find users on the ICQ network, all accessible from the Add/Find Users dialog box. These include

➤ **Find a Random Chat Partner.** Find other ICQ users, randomly. (It's a great way to meet people you weren't looking for!)

➤ **Locate People by Web Directories.** Search for users in over a dozen different online directories. (Unfortunately, these directories list *all* users, including many who aren't ICQ users.)

➤ **ICQ PeopleSpace Directories.** Search for users in the ICQ PeopleSearch directories. (This is probably the best way to search, as the PeopleSpace directories list only ICQ users.)

➤ **White Pages—Similar Interests.** Search the ICQ PeopleSearch directories by interests, background, affiliation, profession, and other similar parameters.

➤ **Users' Public Chat Rooms.** Locate public chat rooms created by other ICQ users.

➤ **View ICQ Users' Lists.** Search a directory of user-created interest lists.

SENDING INSTANT MESSAGES

Once a user is added to your Contact List, it's easy to send an instant message to that user. Just follow these steps:

1. Double-click the user's name in your Contact List.

2. When the Send Message dialog box appears (see Figure 30.3), enter the text of your message in the Enter Message box.

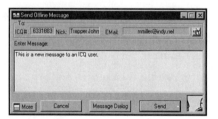

FIGURE 30.3
Sending an instant message to another ICQ user.

3. Click the Send button to send your message.

Your message will be delivered instantly if that user is currently connected to the Internet. If the user is not currently online, the message will be waiting for them when they next log on.

TIP

You can also send files to other ICQ users. To do this, you must run ICQ in *Advanced Mode*. (To select Advanced mode, click the To Advanced Mode button, then click Switch To Advanced Mode.) To send a file, *single-click* the user's name in your Contact List, and select File from the pop-up menu. When the Open dialog box appears, select the file you wish to send, and click OK. When the Send File Request dialog box appears, enter a short description of the file, then click the Send button.

CHATTING WITH ICQ

Sending instant messages back and forth is great, but it's not really real-time conversation. For that, ICQ lets you engage in two-way private chat sessions. These are just like regular chat room sessions, but private, just between the two of you. Follow these steps:

1. *Single-click* the user's name in the Contact List.

2. From the pop-up menu, select ICQ Chat.

3. When the Send Chat Request dialog box appears, enter what you want to talk about in the Enter Chat Subject box, then click Chat.

4. If the user accepts your chat request, a special Chat window will open on your desktop.

5. ICQ Chat works like most other chat services (see Chapter 29, "Chatting with Lycos Chat," for more information). Enter your messages in the bottom message box, and click Enter to send your messages to the chat session. Messages from both users will appear in the main message pane.

If you receive a chat request from another user, a flashing Chat icon will appear in your ICQ window. (If your ICQ window is closed, the flashing icon will appear in your Windows Taskbar tray.) To accept the chat request, double-click on the flashing icon, then select Accept.

ONCE YOU'RE DONE INSTANT MESSAGING...

Now that you've learned how to send and receive real-time instant messages with ICQ, it's time for something completely different. Turn to Chapter 31, "Using FrontPage Express to Create a Web Page," to learn how to create your own personal Web page using Microsoft's FrontPage Express.

CHAPTER 31

USING FRONTPAGE EXPRESS TO CREATE A WEB PAGE

Millions of Web users are becoming content providers—
if only on a small scale. There are several Web communities (such as Tripod, Angelfire, and GeoCities) that exist
solely for the purpose of displaying personal home pages,
and many Internet service providers offer free or low-
charge storage for users' personal Web pages.

In the "old days" (not much more than a year ago, in
Internet time), you had to know how to manually program HTML code in order to create a Web page.
Now, however, FrontPage Express—included free with
Windows 98—makes creating a Web page as easy as
typing and clicking. With FrontPage Express, there is
no messy HTML code to learn.

AN HTML PRIMER

The codes used to create Web pages are part of what is
called **HTML** (HyperText Markup Language). If you
were to see the codes revealed on a Web page, they
would look like words and letters enclosed within angle
brackets, surrounding your visible text. Most codes are in

sets of "on/off" pairs; you turn "on" the code before the text you want to affect, and then turn "off" the code after the text. For example, the code **<H1>** is used to turn specified type into a level-one headline; the code **</H1>** turns off the headline type.

Here are some of the more common HTML codes:

<B>**boldfaces text**</B>

<I>*italicizes text*</I>

<U>underlines text</U>

<TITLE>formats text as the title for your page</TITLE>

TIP

Any piece of text can have multiple codes assigned to it. When multiple codes are used, this is called *nesting*, because the various codes are nested within each other. For example, to italicize title text, the code would look like this: **<TITLE><I>Title Text</I></TITLE>**.

There are other codes that insert items into your page. These codes don't have "on/off" pairs; they're freestanding. These types of codes include:

<P> inserts a paragraph break

**
** inserts a line break

<HR> inserts a horizontal rule

These are just some of the simple codes; you have to use more complex codes to insert a graphic, or to include a hyperlink to another Web page. Fortunately, you don't really have to know these codes to create your own home page—FrontPage Express will do the coding for you!

TIP

Do you really need to know all these HTML codes? If you're using a program like FrontPage Express to create your Web page, the answer is no; these Web page creation programs let you work in a "what you see is what you get" environment and shield you from the underlying coding. However, there are instances where you can benefit from plugging in your own simple HTML code. For example, when you place an ad on the eBay auction site (described in Chapter 20), you can place a plain-text ad, or you can add your own HTML codes to create a colorful and visually interesting ad. For that reason, knowing a few basic HTML codes isn't a bad thing—a nicer looking ad can help you get higher prices for items you have up for bid!

CREATING A WEB PAGE WITH THE PERSONAL HOME PAGE WIZARD

If you want to create your own personal Web page—but don't want to learn HTML coding—Windows 98 includes the perfect tool for your needs. FrontPage Express is a "lite" version of FrontPage, Microsoft's Web page editor that makes creating a Web page just about as easy as desktop publishing a paper in Microsoft Word.

It's easy to create a simple personal Web page with FrontPage Express; a special Wizard leads you through all the steps. Just follow these instructions:

1. Click the Start button, select Programs, select Internet Explorer, and then select FrontPage Express.

2. When FrontPage Express launches, pull down the File menu and select New.

3. When the New Page dialog box appears, select Personal Home Page Wizard and click OK.

TIP

In addition to the Personal Home Page Wizard, there are also Wizards to create other types of pages—including survey and confirmation forms.

4. When the first screen of the Personal Home Page Wizard appears (see Figure 31.1), select the sections you want to appear on your home page, and then click <u>N</u>ext.

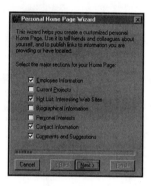

FIGURE 31.1
Use the Personal Home Page Wizard to create your own personal Web page.

5. Follow the remaining on-screen instructions to complete your personal home page.

6. When the final screen appears, click <u>F</u>inish.

FrontPage Express now generates the HTML code for your page and displays the resulting page in its main window (see Figure 31.2).

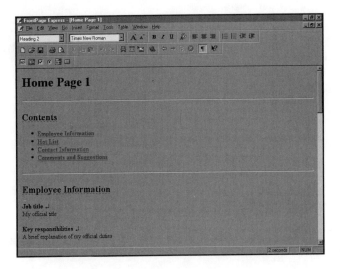

FIGURE 31.2

After you complete the Personal Home Page Wizard, FrontPage Express auto-matically generates your own personal Web page.

CHANGING TEXT ATTRIBUTES

Once you've entered text into your new Web page, you're left with a fairly ugly-looking Web page, comprised of nothing but boring text. Fortunately, you can spruce up that text with a variety of special visual attributes—all accessible from the FrontPage Express toolbar (shown in Figure 31.3).

1. Highlight the text you wish to modify.

2. To apply a different style, select a style from the Change Style drop-down list.

3. To change the font, select a new font from the Change Font drop-down list.

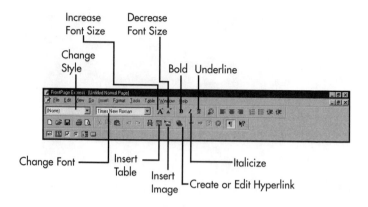

Increase Font Size

Decrease Font Size

Change Style

Bold Underline

Change Font — Insert Table

Insert Image

Italicize

Create or Edit Hyperlink

FIGURE 31.3
Use the FrontPage Express toolbar to add special formatting to your basic Web page.

4. To change type size, click either the Increase Font Size or Decrease Font Size buttons.

5. To boldface the text, click the Bold button.

6. To italicize the text, click the Italicize button.

7. To underline the text, click the Underline button.

TIP

Use underlining sparingly, because hyperlinked text is automatically underlined; any non-hyperlinked text you underlined could be confused with hyperlinked text.

8. To change the color of the text, click the Text Color button and select a color from the Color dialog box.

9. To make the selected text a numbered list, click the Numbered List button.

10. To make the selected text a bulleted list, click the
Bulleted List button.

As you can see, changing text attributes in your Web page
is very similar to changing text attributes in Microsoft
Word—select the text, then click the appropriate button
on the toolbar.

CREATING HYPERLINKS

A *hyperlink* is a link to another Web page—another one of
your pages, or another page on another Internet site.
When a user clicks on a hyperlink, he or she is taken
directly to the linked page.

Hyperlinks allow you to link to additional information
without having to include that information directly on
your page. For example, if you're creating a page about
computer books, you could create a link to one of the
many online bookstores, such as www.barnesandnoble.com
or www.amazon.com; this way users can access these sites
directly from your page, just by clicking the hyperlink.

Follow these steps to add a hyperlink to your FrontPage
Express Web page:

> **TIP**
>
> If, in your text, you type a standard Web address (starting with
> either http:// or www), FrontPage Express will automatically
> create a hyperlink for that address.

1. Highlight the text you wish to link to another page.

2. Click the Create Hyperlink button.

3. When the Create Hyperlink dialog box appears, select the World Wide Web tab, type the address of the other page into the URL box, then click OK.

TIP

If you wish to link to an existing page on your own site, select the Open Pages tab and choose a page from the Open Pages list.

Once you create a hyperlink, it will appear on your page underlined and in blue.

ADDING GRAPHICS

Plain-text Web pages are boring; spruce up the look of your Web page with pictures. Follow these steps:

1. Position the cursor where you wish to insert the graphic.

2. Click the Insert Image button.

3. When the Image dialog box appears, select the Other Location tab, select From File, and enter the location of the graphics file to insert.

4. Click OK when done.

The graphics file will now appear at the insertion point. To edit the properties of the picture—including how it is positioned on the page, and how text wraps around it—right-click the image, select Image Properties, and configure the appropriate options in the Image Properties dialog box.

ADDING OTHER COMPONENTS WITH WEBBOTS

FrontPage Express automates the creation of many advanced components with a special "mini-wizard" called a *WebBot*. For example, you can use the WebBot to create a search form on your Web page, or insert a timestamp. Just follow these steps:

1. Position the cursor where you wish to insert the new component.

2. Click the WebBot button.

3. When the Insert WebBot Component dialog box appears, select the component you wish to insert. For purposes of this task, select Search and click OK.

4. When the WebBot Search Component Properties dialog box appears, modify the appropriate fields and click OK.

If FrontPage Express didn't include the WebBot, you'd have to code all these special components by hand, which is no easy chore!

TIP

FrontPage Express includes only a limited number of WebBots. For a more complete selection of these special components, check out the full retail version of the program, FrontPage 97.

ONCE YOU'VE CREATED YOUR WEB PAGE...

Now that you've created your own personal Web page, you have to post it to a Web site. Proceed to Chapter 32, "Placing Personal Web Pages with Tripod and Angelfire," to learn how to post your pages to one of many popular community Web sites.

CHAPTER 32

PLACING PERSONAL WEB PAGES WITH TRIPOD AND ANGELFIRE

In the last chapter, you learned how to use FrontPage Express to create your own personal Web pages. Once you've created your Web pages, you need to post them on a server so that other Web users can access them. To do that, you need to find a service that serves as a host for personal Web pages.

Many Internet Service Providers (and America Online) will let you post your pages on their servers. But there are also special Web "communities" that specialize in hosting personal Web pages. Two of these communities are associated with Lycos: Tripod and Angelfire.

TIP

Tripod and Angelfire are just two of many different personal Web page communities. Other popular communities include GeoCities (www.geocities.com) and The Globe (www.the-globe.com).

ALL ABOUT TRIPOD AND ANGELFIRE

Tripod and Angelfire are both communities of personal Web pages. Both let you post Web pages created with FrontPage Express and other programs; both offer their own programs to create your own home pages; and both are free services. Yet each of these services have their own individual personality.

Tripod (www.tripod.com) is one of the largest home page communities on the Web, with close to two million users, four million individual Web pages, and more than a hundred different "pod" communities. Tripod's home pages and communities are organized into the following topic "zones": Cars&Trucks, Computers, Entertainment, Fun&Games, Health/Fitness, Home/Family, Jobs/Career, Money/Business, Shopping, Society/Culture, Sports, Teens, Travel, and Women. Tripod is very much about the "community experience," with lots of chat rooms, message boards, and newsletters to help you communicate with other members with similar interests.

Angelfire (www.angelfire.com) is less about community, and more about professional-looking Web pages. While Tripod is great for the casual Web user or hobbyist with a personal page or two, Angelfire is better for more professional pages from individuals, small businesses, or community organizations. Angelfire does not group pages into "communities" or "zones" or "pods;" you simply get your URL and you're on your own.

TIP

In addition to going through the individual Tripod or Angelfire services, you can also create a simple homepage directly from

Lycos. Go to pagebuilder.lycos.com and select from one of the pre-defined Web page templates. Complete the forms online and you'll create a very basic Web page, which will then be placed on the Tripod service. If you want a more sophisticated page, bypass this Lycos Free Homepage service and go directly to either Tripod or Angelfire.

CREATING AND POSTING PAGES ON TRIPOD

Tripod makes it easy to become a member (free of charge) and create or post your personal Web pages. Just follow these steps:

1. Go to the main Tripod Web page at www.tripod.com. (See Figure 32.1.)

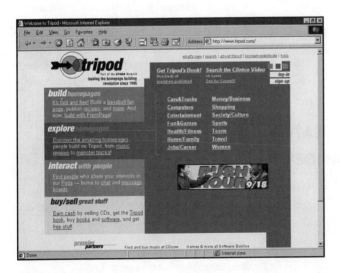

FIGURE 32.1
Join a community of personal Web pages at Tripod (www.tripod.com).

2. If this is your first visit, click the sign-up link and fill out the following Sign Up page. Click the Submit button when finished to register your membership.

3. When the next page appears, click the "pods" you wish to join, then click the Submit button.

4. When the next page appears, fill in any appropriate "pod" information, then click the Submit button.

5. Return to the Tripod home page and click the build homepages link.

6. To create a simple home page with Tripod's Homepage Builder, click the quick page link and follow the onscreen instructions.

7. To create a more sophisticated home page, click the custom builder link and follow the onscreen instructions.

8. To upload pages created with another program (such as FrontPage Express), click the housekeeper link and follow the onscreen instructions.

Once your main Web page is created, Tripod will assign a unique Web page address (URL) to your page.

CREATING AND POSTING PAGES ON ANGELFIRE

Using Angelfire is similar to using Tripod, although there are more options available for advanced Web page creators. Just follow these steps to create a home page at Angelfire:

1. Go to the main Angelfire Web page at www.angelfire.com. (See Figure 32.2.)

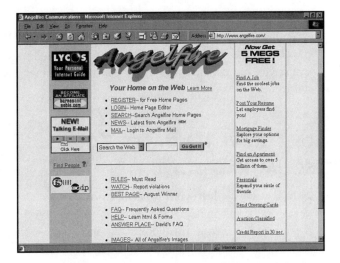

FIGURE 32.2
Getting right down to business with Angelfire (www.angelfire.com).

2. Click the REGISTER link and fill out the Register page. Click the Send the Information button to register your membership.

3. When the Make A Home page appears, select a home state, enter a directory name, enter a password, then click the Send the Information button.

4. When the Friendly Reminder page appears, click the Create Your Free Home Page NOW button.

5. Use Angelfire's Basic Editor to create a basic home page. Click the View Your Page button to preview your page.

6. To activate your page, click the Submit Your Page button.

7. You are now presented with the Web Shell page. Use this page to make changes to your pages—and upload any pages you created with another Web page editor.

To upload previously created pages or to edit existing Angelfire pages, go to the main Angelfire page and click the LOGIN link. This will take you to the Web Shell page, where you can perform all sorts of editing tasks, including uploading pages.

ONCE YOU'VE UPLOADED YOUR PERSONAL PAGES...

Now that you've learned how to place your personal pages on Tripod and Angelfire, you've learned everything there is to know from this book. You can now close the covers, put the book someplace handy (just in case you need to look something up in the future), grab your mouse, and do some serious Web surfing!

TIP

If you want to learn even more about the Internet or creating Web pages, check out the complete selection of books at the Macmillan Computer Publishing Web site (www.mcp.com). If you want to see some of the other books written by this author, check out my personal Web site at www.macmillanusa.com/people/miller. If you want to contact me with comments or questions, feel free to email me at mmiller@mcp.com. If you just want to get on with your Web surfing, quit reading right now and get to it!

INDEX

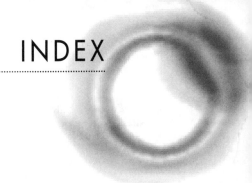

X-Z